AF266193

THE OPULENCE OF INVENTION

THE OPULENCE OF INVENTION

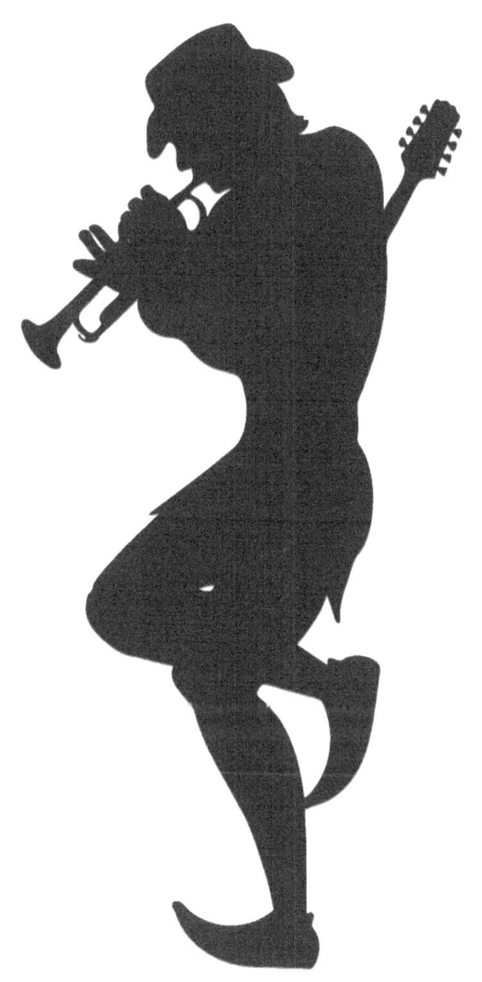

E. P. MATTSON

ISBN: 978-0-9993982-0-3
Library Of Congress Control Number: 2017913998

Acknowledgments
A section of text is reprinted from the short story
Silver Blaze by Arthur Conan Doyle.
Photograph: Eleven Men With Beards, Top Hats,
and Vests, 1848-1855, half-plate daguerreotype,
photographer unknown.

Seeker Savior
848 N Rainbow Blvd. #3558
Las Vegas, NV 89107

1st paperback edition 2018
10 9 8 7 6 5 4 3 2 1

For Mom and Dad

Contents

The World Is Flat

Ladies and gentlemen, direct your attention,
a device with importance we hardly need mention.
It pounces, parades, jockeys and jettisons,
slamming doors locking the salesman *in.*

Ubiquitous treats, circuitous streets,
ruinous, torturous, squeezing your eyes
in a glass vice of lies, a dark church of vice
painting a portrait of flypaper flies.

Observe in its wiles how it teasingly tries
to invoke your libido, (that is its credo).
Enticing with icing, always surprising,
a mistake that's carving your mind like a cake!

    The spirit retreats from calamitous curs,
    from jackboots and spurs, conducting the herds,
    calling the heifers, we all follow after
    chewing our grass in the glass of disaster.

Like magic show puppets, or bodies of hide
we come alive for the hand that reaches inside,
massaging our organs with dexterous fingers
engenders malaise, and ennui lingers.

    Narcotic mantra, a skeletal dancer,
    a wasteland of glass, an orchard of ash,
    a Cyclops that snatches at kids as they pass.

Admen sold on the yellow brick road
paving our old and flaccid, acid-fed
minds of tin and hay, and Dorothy's
come-hither so invitingly fey, her
pucker pink with the promise of power

so we shower in poppy dust hour by
hour. Relaxing, non-taxing, creatively
blasting our freewill to ruins, our
language to jargon.

A bargain you say? It's free, I agree.
Though cable's enabled the rise of the fee.
The flickering channels beckon us all
to a circus of mirthless and stalled bacchanals.

> *Listen my children and you shall hear*
> *of the white noise of fear, the cries of despair.*
> *They call it programming, don't you agree?*
> *A robot can't walk without a decree.*

So what'll it be my delicious confections,
the charming erection who won the election?
Or perhaps just the rantings of temporal thieves
spitting up morphine, stealing our dreams,
our faces awash in a glowing collision
fattened like pigs, lobotomized citizens.

The choices are few but pay them their due,
for coffers were spent to give you the cue.
And like wine from the grape, with teeth
at our nape, we've all come to gape
at the mass mind rape.

But for those who believe that lying is wrong
that hearts still beat strong in the light of the sun
the choice is still yours, the day is still young
the meadows still green, the rivers still run
awaiting you all in the kingdom of nature
can you still hear the call from your
living room pasture?

The door's within reach
You've still got your hands
Your fidgeting feet still obey your commands
Your coma subsides, you've found out you're alive!
Will you waste one more day
in your living room hive?

The clock has stopped ticking
The door's open wide
Run outside
   Run outside
      Run outside
         RUN OUTSIDE!

The Origin Of Dreams

Way down the sightless, slumbering wastes
of a moonless mind, anchored in the hollow
like a thumbnail crab in the pink slides
of a conch's heart, awaits a silver sailing ship
of solitary, drowning voyages
borne on currents of rushing memory.

Once nightly, there steals a flashing spine
of light, forged from realization
piercing blue rolling waves and streaking
through undersea mountains.

This illumined eel invades the subconscious
and corrals all thought into a whirling torrent
whipping the helm clockwise and releasing
the sleeping barge from ancient reefs of fear.

In this way, the ship roams a lifetime of years.

The 40 Mile Desert Crossing
To California, 1849

We all went west.

                  Hawks sail high over the ridge
             inspecting our marching
          insect procession
       melting into the alkali desert
moth eyes mired in diamond pools of unwater.

Spiny mountain crags cast long blue shadows
       over this white waste of sand.
A crew of loons, a stew of wounds
      horses mules oxen
         heat thirst starvation
            men becoming dunes.

Ox skulls stare with cavernous holes
         cobwebs strangling wooden wheels
      caked in dust under horseless wagons.

      The cry of the Overlanders
       `another ox down'

He took my wife for an angel
licking ten trembling dew drops
from her fine, pouring fingers.
His weight wed the ground
and his shoulders stiffened slightly,
one more final morning under the searing desert sky.

The Reverend James Welsh Brier and Company
    set out on the Southern route today

waved their withered wings
exited the stage and altered the dream.

But then the mad reverend raged
                and seizing the stage
        flew his Jayhawks west
                with flour scoops raised
        in the haze
of a valley named death.

        The cry of the Overlanders
          `another ox down'

Five days gone,
    and the manifest urge, like a dirge
        calls our maddening hive of
                        l
                         i
                          t
                          t
                          e
                        r
                        ing lives
                spilling out in a tiring tide
        where the walking dead
                drag passed
                        the dark
                unseen fork
        to the guidebook meadows.

It's man's fate to seek,
make steel of his body
and gold of his heart,
we tear up the path behind us,
clambering into the dreams of red men.

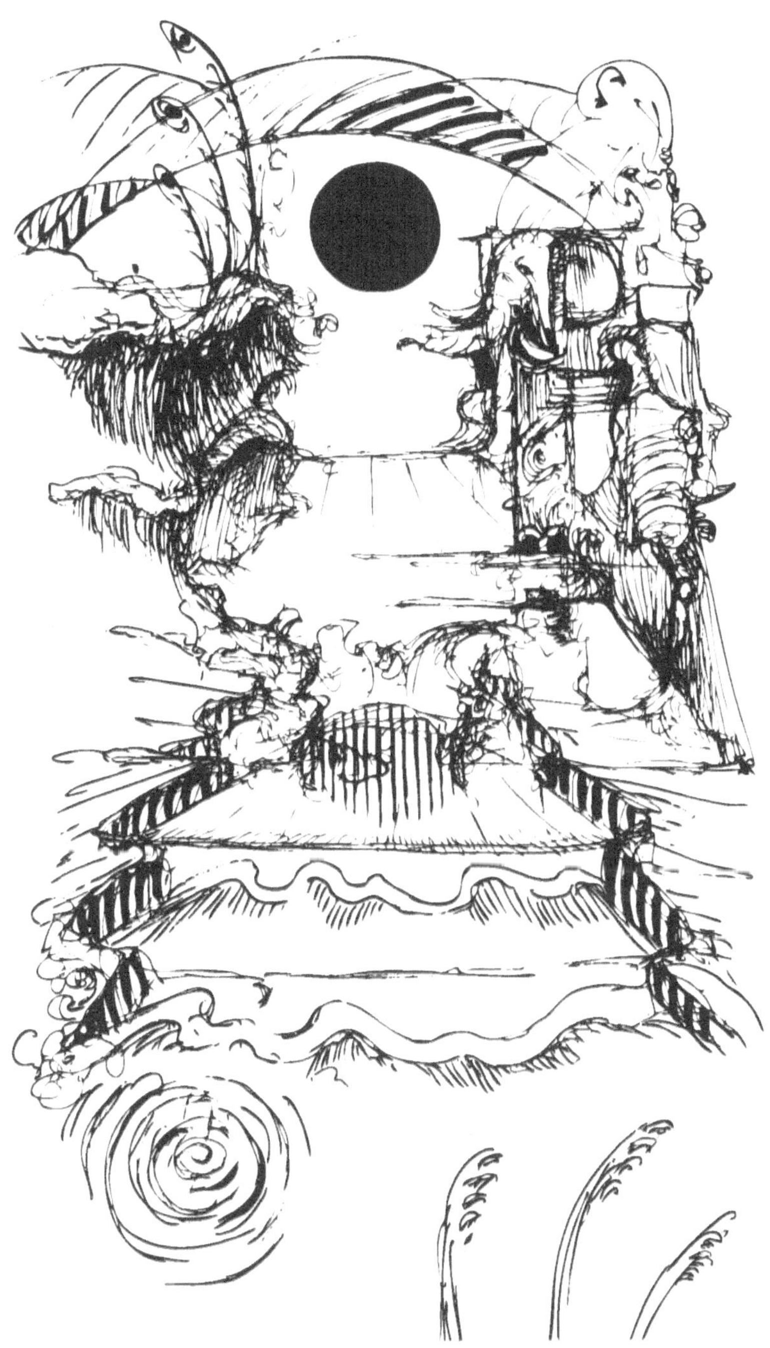

OUR TOP HATS ARE RAILROAD NAILS!
Ask yer ascot, it'll tell ya square. As mayor of
starch I bequeath the land beneath my feet for
me! Each and every livery range is pocket
change, a feed of green where the shitter doth
gleam with a gatherin' steam. Indeed is a
deed decreed (from a quill of black blood)
that the madhatter mothers will have their
druthers of Malakoff mud! Quid pro quo and
the party of the first part. Blankety-blank to
yer territories, arrows & savage injun hearts.
You'd like more metaphors here ya go, there's
a beak in my belly my heart is a crow. BLIM!
BLAM! BLAST! CRUNCH! A cannon of
water, a gambler's hunch. Ya ain't never seen
no spunkier penguin than a barroom
bumpkin in velveteen, so we'll expose
ourselves to the man with the glass and
yuze can savor the sweetness of class.
YOUR LAND TO US IS FATED, GOLD-PLATED & SEDATED
UNTIL THE DAY WE'RE SATED. BY GUM WE'RE ALL RELATED!

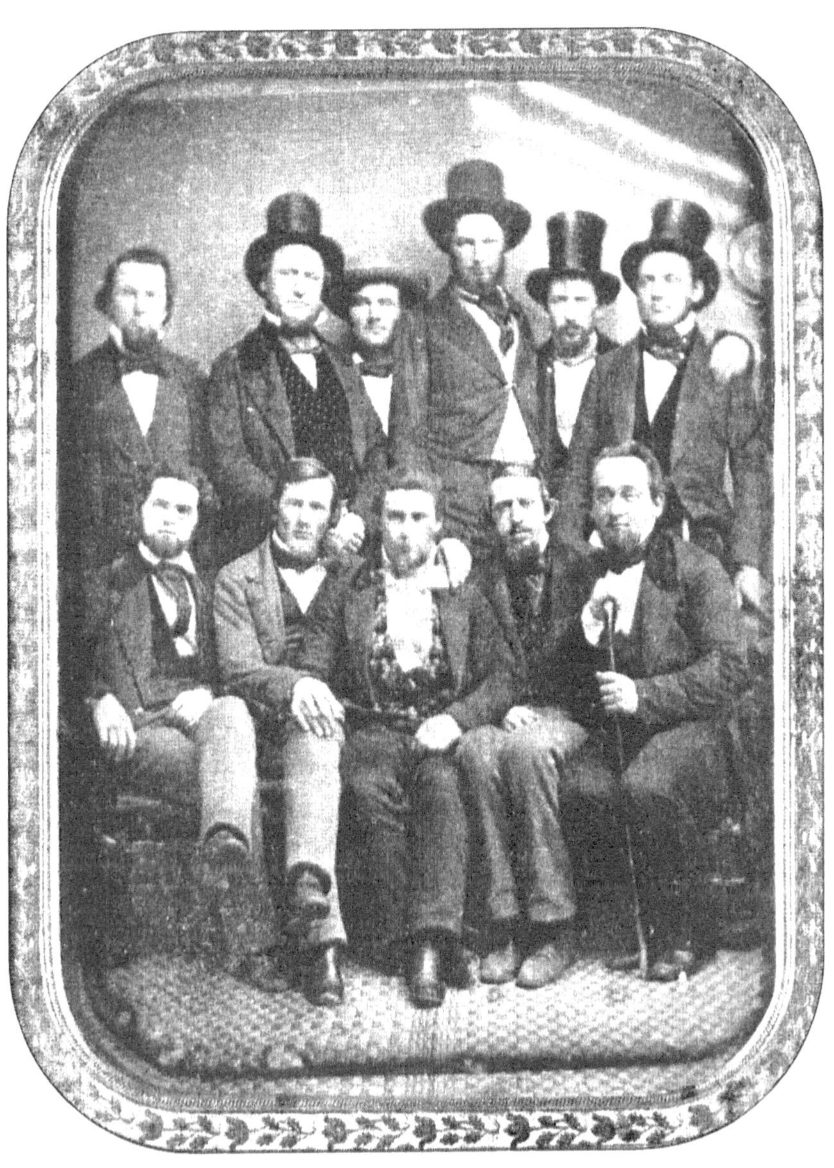

The Belles Of The Barbary Coast

In the year of 1849, the pirates came all soaked in brine.
The young and old, they all heard told
of tales of pans and the promised gold.

But that got old, so they changed their plans
sold off their gear to some other man
and with industrious druthers stayed on with the others
to build up the land on the fine 'Frisco sand.

And rowdies wrecked on Laudanum
found fame on Maiden Lane.
Looking in lust to lift up some bustles
(and aching to hustle), they staggered
down gambling dens for a fill of fine amber venom
and losing all wisdom, were craftily led
to dark shanty shacks
where their fate they awaited
where the water got black.

Face-to-face they were with a red-headed fella
name of Shanghai Kelly, who'd offer a toast.
The barbarous host of the Barbary Coast
would, (in jovial manner), offer the stammering drunks
a dunk for a fix, (a drink concocted of opium tricks),
and after a sip, without much decor, the dumb
drunken sods fell right through the floor!

Plummeting, clutching thin air, they went down.
Falling through rafters to dark, hidden freighters
and sent off to sea all cadaverous cold,
waking on waves the next bleary morning
spitting and heaving, their bloated faces showing
their sad loss of grace, for without any haste

this boatload of lives was shipped off to far off
Shanghai on the tides. Their cries met no favor,
so long to the sailors.

And then in the 50's when wild vixens ruled
a hornet's nest of burlesque-questing drunkards
caught pox on the docks pursuing perfume.
The loons all made trysts and traded quick kisses,
blinding their visages, and thrilling to girls in fair,
flowing dresses. They'd follow them home
seeking mad sin, hacking and sneaking,
and reeking of gin.

> *And the men clawed the women*
> *and the women would swoon*
> *for goons in saloons*
> *under big, yellow moons.*

But finally one day, near the end of the year
a pair of portly, adroit politicians
concocted a mission of visions severe.
(Observing this gaity without much morality),
they entered the fray, and having their way
the Abatement Act of `17
ended all the seamen's dreams
for Rolph & Hearst were in cahoots
to fire the pretty prostitutes.

O O O O O O O O O O O O O O O O

[   ]

shakespeare sputtered in the guttering summer
licking a lager lizardlike, foam trickling
down
his
bard
beard
guffawing like a horse mad
heroic oedipus wreck, wooing women
with wine & fine crafted lines growing like vines
curling into weedlions and roaring at the stage
of bianca shrewing violets.

Photograph In a Museum

Little gypsy child
    your tambourine rings its teeth
of clattering coins
    hypnotizing the dimensional executioner.

A black velvet hat
    docks on your pale expression
and a wave of whitecaps
    tumbles down your sister's Sunday dress.

Your face, filled with white nightmares
    your stare, mercury-etched
        upon a silver salver sits
            steadied by curatorial fingertips.

Study For A Phantasm
-for Salvador Dali

Shadows stroke the melting landscape.
Dali, the gaunt guide of lazy time
grows spiral horns, his horse ribs
caging the rabbit heart of silence.

Shadows meander over the land

atavistic ants with jittering mandibles

flapping crows make black hieroglyphics

curdling curtains of tattered clouds

dripping skies puddling in placid lakes

of mirroring mercury, reflecting crepuscular castles

gleaming with phosphorescent scales.

Man of melting continents
   stretches dream skin
in a somnambulist egg birth
   of red suicide.

Under the dripping arachnid canopy
the inquisitor woman fountain
caresses the sliding marble periscope
cracking with flowers, bleeding musk
birthing the mayhem of daylight.

Out here, crutches run like naked scarecrows
littering this vast surrealist continuum...

-: A :-
-: N :-
-: D :-
| T |
| H |
| R |
| O |
| U |
| G |
| H |
this topography
our hero rides a
disappearing
desiccated
steed into
the languid
haze of a skeletal
orchestral apparition
becoming a guitar.
|

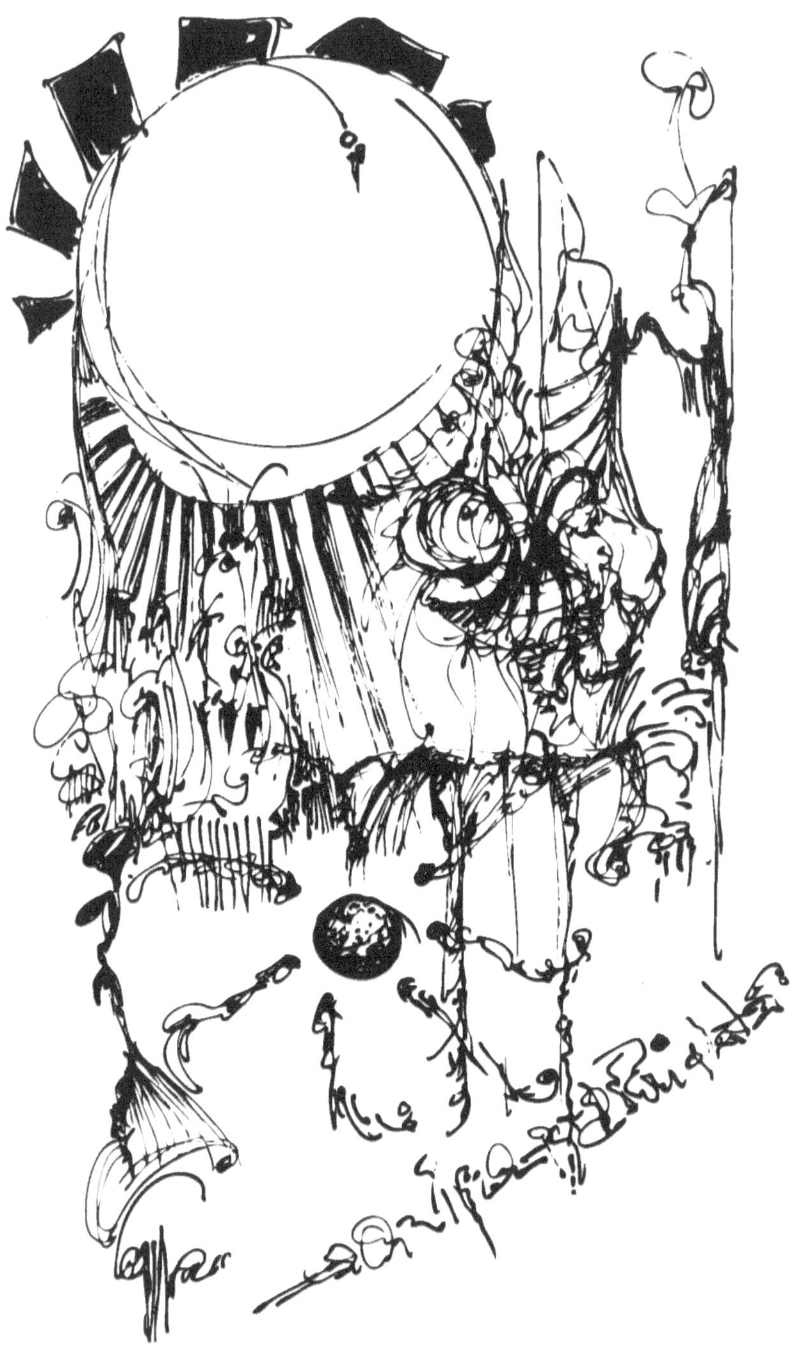

Schoolyard Stanzas
-for Salvador Dali

The Pharmacist Of Ampurdan
  devours the crumbling marzipan
misplaces his monocle in the sand
  The Pharmacist Of Ampurdan.

Venus de Milo With Her Drawers
  bows in plaster to the wandering hordes
negates the need for furniture mores
  Venus de Milo With Her Drawers.

The drone of the Lobster Telephone
  nibbling numbers Nairobi to Nome
the operator whispers crustaceous moans
  The drone of the Lobster Telephone.

Three Fried Eggs Without The Plate
  conspire in deed to sublimate
breakfasting antics to something romantic
  Three Fried Eggs Without The Plate.

Swans Reflecting Elephants
  a menagerie of swanephants
an idyllic, phallic, oasis séance
  Swans Reflecting Elephants.

A Couple With Their Heads Full Of Clouds
  dine in the desert and wonder aloud
contained in a frame for the logical crowds
  A Couple With Their Heads Full Of Clouds.

H o r n e t   H o n e y
"The honeybees with their golden honey,
the hornets with their white honey."
-Jean Follain

Spreading painfully
  on shuddering crumb cakes
it maims the palette
  harvested by hard-time criminals
it blackens the tongue.

A sticky improbable dew
  that eats away sugar
and drinks up the tea
  when spooned into teacups
leaving a waste of pain.

It's no pleasant morning milking,
  the stripes, black and yellow
force their sharpened bodies
  in newborn holes like aeromoles.

It takes a hundred hours
  to fill a small jar.
Such a delicacy,
   they each are milked
individually.

And as is the lot of the fantastic
  this salve can't be got with the ease of a claret.
One trifling vial, its bouquet of bile,
  solely the nectar of poets.

The Moon

That great balloon in the sky
land of blue heliotropes
hosts midnight-mad revelers
dancing under jellyfish parasols.

Lusty lunar maids
writhe in green sea foam
toss plundered abalone
to their fine, fetching feet
that gleam in the glittering sand.

Comets run aground,
and crater crabs sidle to the sea.

Celestial children call the leviathan,
swirling the oceans with long curling arms
conducting astral rain.

And the sky comes alive with fireflies
        swarming into galaxies
                and Martians arrive by the millions
to join in this astral cotillion,
        while the wandering stars snooze
                meandering in blue
and me and you aim our telescopes true
        stealing the secrets of heaven.

Fanfare For The Postmoderns

Half mad forms
splattered on an easel's pasture
are stillborn, yet feign rapture
on the walls of modern architecture.

A tempting trail of mating,
indentured academia
flaking-off, but correlating.

Licking shoes, twice entombed
        in a maze of white rooms
    the intellectuals swoon
            they're strolling in time
    as they purr and they croon
            for a place in line
    behind the latest art crime.

For to reject is to doom a possible boon
to the marching egos marinating in gloom.
`Why, mankind is a blight drilling down into grime,
we must echo our descent with inventions of mind!'
And the artist? `Divine! Ahead of his time!'

Or is it all just hallelujah moonshine?

Asylum Of Birds
-for Max Ernst

Forests of riddles coalesce
into castles of wax, temples of flesh.
Earthquake footfalls announce
his marching form, mashing mushrooms
crushing corn, a stride of miles
defies his trials, born for a brush and a vial.

Captured in France, a surrealist guest
a questionable bird in a factory's nest
at the venomous Vichy police's behest.
An artistic stance in duress may suggest
the metaphysical dance of chess.

Embracing arms of empty arabesques
release their hollow suitors.
Nightingales in bridal veils, the feathered Rubenesque
sequestered courtesans, dutifully doting
tugging at their molting décolletage
ordered by collapse of his grattage.

Colors marry form to divine the unknown
but Max's light shines
through our cathedral of minds
collapsing our dreams
freeing clocks from our rooms.

Nightmare landscapes, *blinding moons.*

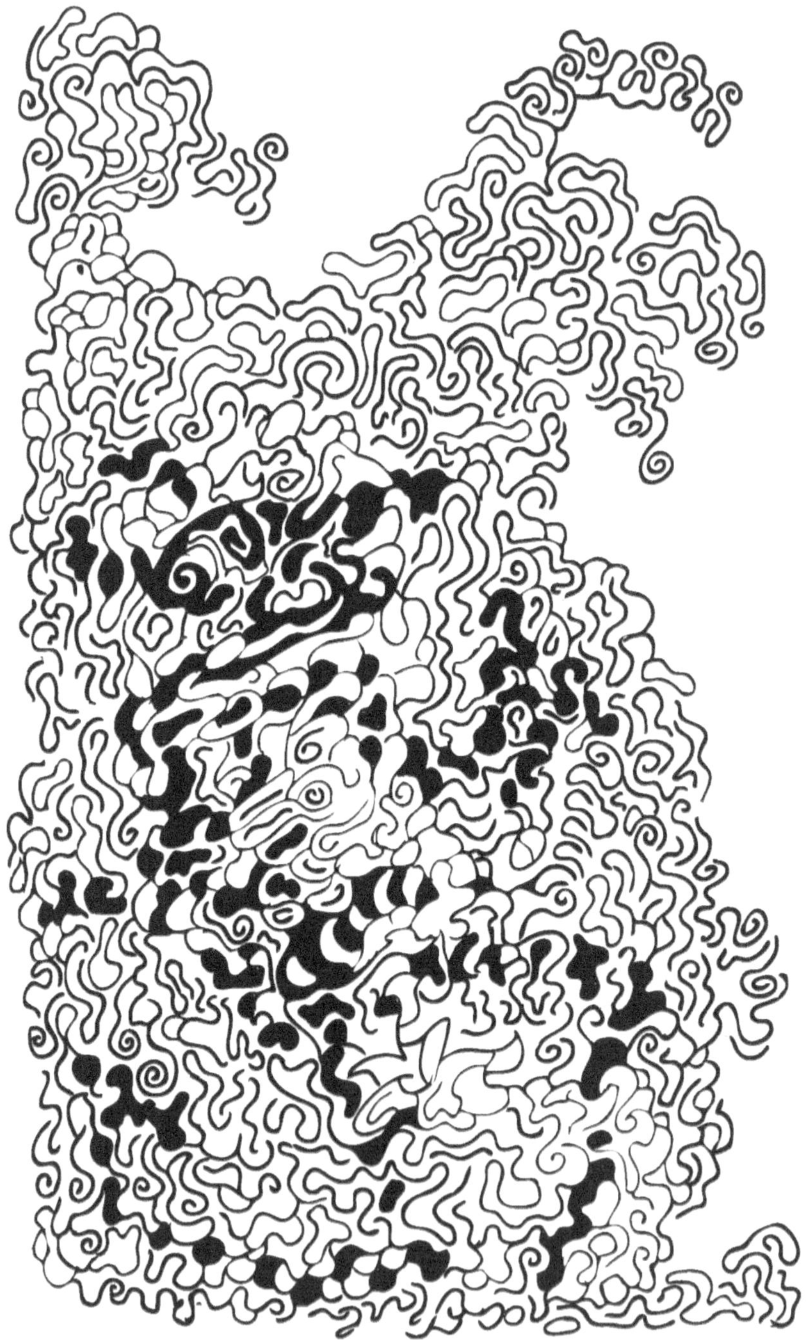

Black Writing

The paper blinds like a white narcotic
one acre of snow
burying crops in tabula rasa.

I scratch at the pale earth
with an ink hoe, a crow of words
tilling the page with a black talon.

Animal tracks scurry cryptically
leashed to the seismographic needle
sketching subconscious tremors.

Walking west to the sun
kicking up buried orchards
the crops rise behind and sprout crooked branches
laden with watching birds.

I look back -
a salt pillar at the edge of the world.

Visions Of A Rainforest

I. Lime, fruit of fountains
   oval vial of forest perfume
   verdant egg of peeling armor
   drained in sour rivers.

II. Panda peering
   cloud with coal eyes
   paws clawing bamboo shoots
   flutes in a white mind.

III. Terrestrial tarantula
   creeping crooked braids
   swinging on the jaguar's tail
   eyeing the chittering marmoset.

IV. Stout, grunting boar
   bellowing blood of warfare
   muscular, waddling root-grubber
   brood of tusk horses
   gargoyle of ground.

V. Golden buzzing violins
   dizzily diving bloom shepherds
   pollen pirates, knights of nectar
   zebra motes of honey dust.

VI. Tired little gypsy
   with her cloak of rainbows
   cawing axe of horn
   craning on the rubber tree
   her pigment garment
   fanning in fervent spears.

VII.   Under the green forest canopy
        in the dark heart of the earth
        roam these exotic visions of life
        singing their mad, perfect song
        in the last meadows of shadow.

Hamburger Hamburger Jiggity Jig

(An apple pie occasion of a jungle home invasion)

Lolloping, trolloping scissory saws
        deadgroundcow
        deadgroundcow
Tumbling the green for our jittery jaws
        deadgroundcow
        deadgroundcow

                Axiom of axes
              Loraxian apocalypse
          a copse of trees, a ravenous plow
          hamburger hamburger jiggity jig
      RAZE THE LAND AND LOWER THE COWS!

Down come the monkeys, two by two
    their souls make their way to Solla Sollew
        only shadows where the parrots once flew
    down they come, down they come, tigresses too
collected and crated and shipped to a zoo.

           Pickle & onion deforestation
          quarter-pound annihilation
        lizardly, scissory sesame saws
      RAZE THE LAND AND LOWER THE COWS!

Corporations see gold through yellow-tinted glasses
    surveying the wasteland burning in ashes
        numbering their lumbering cattle in jeeps
           the underlings log all the bovine receipts
        while the rare waste away in museums of meat
    and the clawing exotics all come to their ends
those dim-witted beasts have such powerful friends!

Paradise has seen its fall
Eden
then nothing at all.
Reason slows to a crawl
in faces full of
Phenobarbital.

That's all folks, it's been swell
the heifers head after the sawing dinner bell.
The dried-up old stumps that once held eyes
don't sprout no sprigs.

Hamburger hamburger jiggity jig
magnificent kingdom of grandeur and green
now barren, obscene with new grazing tenants,
a desolate greed devoid of all sense
inhaled at the drive-thru for 99 cents.

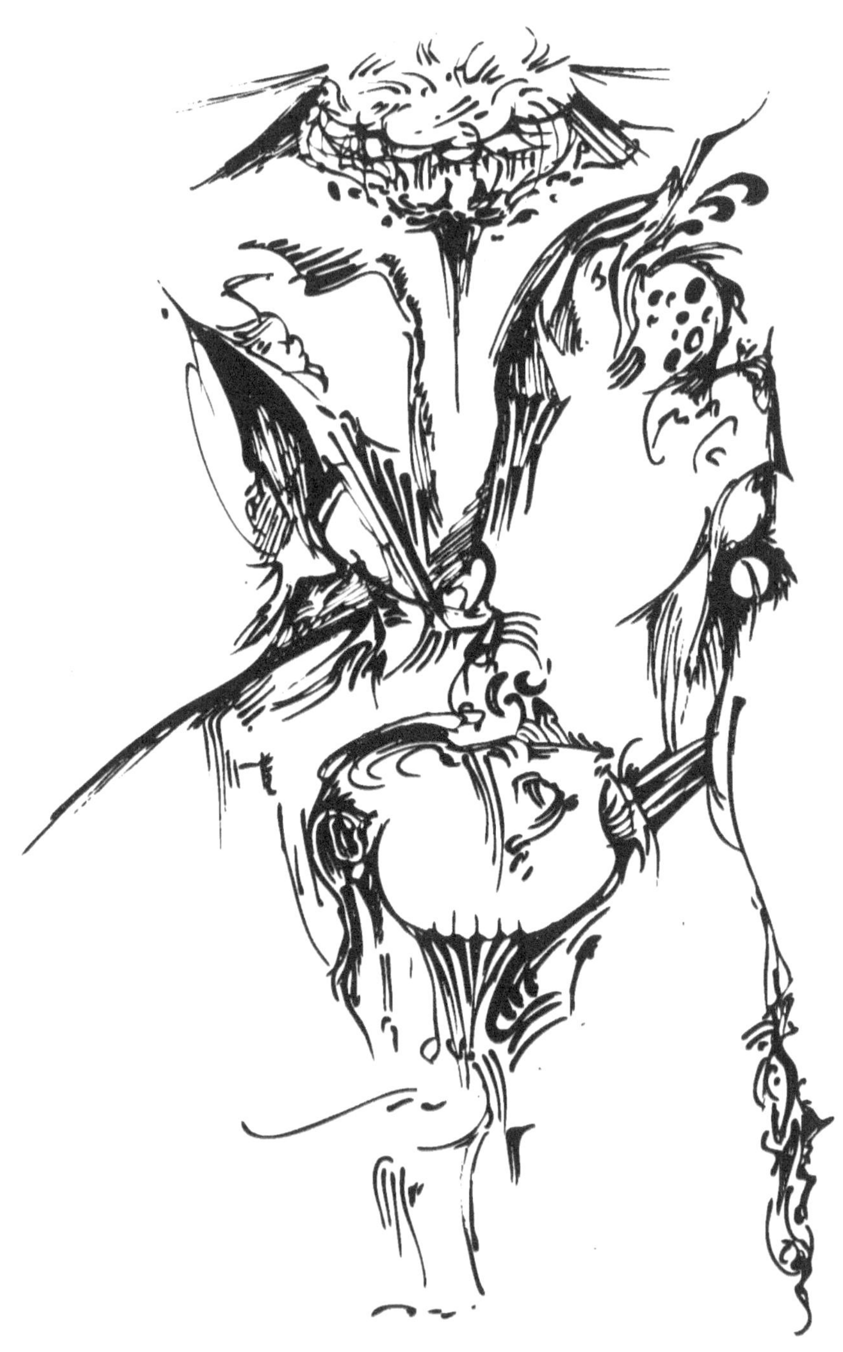

Suburbia Vs. The Mountain Lion

The
suburban home
stealthily encircles the
mountain lion. There is a feint

of junk mail. Suddenly, a snapping feline fang punctures the mailbox! The crowd *gasps* as the automatic garage door crushes a straying paw. The lion falters! The house leaps like a killing swan catching its foe's snout in a twisting sewer grate. Desperate claws scratch aluminum siding, cat teeth shattering in silence. A snaking garden hose worms its way into biting lion jaws flooding gullet with distilled water. Drowning eyes wild with extinction roll back like blinking slot machines, and the house *roars*, gutters curling ecstatically. The supporting wall beheads its kill and picket fences gather the lion's pride. The crowd *cheers* as the house stuffs the mewling babes down its chimney maw. And with garden shear ceremony,

the
flayed
mother's pelt
is fitted
to the
front steps.

Scene From a Film

In *The Horseman On The Roof*
        ravenous crows fed like locusts
                on bodies dead with Cholera.

Battling black brothers stealing
        eyes, skin, entrails
they settled like shrouds in the kitchens
                of provincial towns.

As I remember it, their wings
        fluttered like the dark hair
                of a running woman
        when our hero flung the door open
                to each neighborhood mausoleum
        revolted in the face of such
chaotic ravenous greed.

But the soldiers of obsidian
        screamed once in agitation
                and returned as a nation
        to feed.

M a y a   D e r e n

Maya Deren, archer of sight
navigating the prison of stairwells
her shadow eludes her own desire
and like a cat she claws her own subconscious.

Crawling toward truth
selling solace for the price of driftwood
her dress carved by light and shadow
a canopy of lovely womanhood.

In the palms of the businessmen crawl maggots of fear,
they feast on erratic movements, gathered at long tables.
Maya arrives unnoticed, while egos fight over cutlets.

   See Time pursue Maya with the sluggishness of stone
   shattering her portrait in shards at the beach.

Her backward-dancing films seem to suggest
that we live in a sanitarium of marionettes.
Retreating waves pulling shells to the depths.
And Death is just a suitor for lonely coquettes,
his face mirrors their dashed hopes
as he collects them in his robes.

   If grapes are the infants of wine,
   Maya is the infant of Satori.

And I see now that time is a locket
hung on eternity's neck.

Kneel Before Jod
-for Alejandro Jodorowsky

Jodorowski, shaman of the pre-hysteric mind
Standing before a black hole, arms raised
Vomiting rainbows from the mouth of a camera
Images flood like psychedelic lava
Flowing through the birth canal of our minds.

A butterfly in a caterpillar prison
Illustrates a solitary ideal
That ideas are the insects of achievement
Set aloft by chromatic, galactic wings.

Buñuel's death dinner
Explodes in a thousand crystal shards.
Metaphors harden and stand at attention
Blindfolded before machine gun fire
Shot from the unerring hand of empire.

When ideas bow to the shrine of conformity
When art eats itself to survive
The inhumane reptilian brain will celebrate
Revealing its scales before the original creator.

Film reels infused with the post-sexual musk
Of plundered beauty, depict a ghastly tableau:
Quivering mountains of meat
Lakes of blood under dangling innocents
Architects of insanity dancing slow waltzes
With the descendants of tortured beef.
Behold their snouts of serpentine design
Sniffing their burning brothers in carnal ecstasy.

With inverted eyes, Jodorowski seems to mock
               ~ our collective dream ~
`O sorrow fanatic, drama devotee, oracle of hurricanes,
Can you not see that you stand as a meat monolith
Blocking all your unsung Edison proclamations?
You are your own worst enemy turning in on itself!
A hobo ouroboros with its tail in its pie hole
Cowering in fear before the lifting veil.'

> *But when the mind fragments, its pieces can gather*
> *Like broken clay pots forming future messiahs.*

`My friend, take your torch, your phaser, your trumpet.
Call to your brothers, they are not zombies!
They are as you, they are the apples of Nostradamus.
Ply them with fine liquors, and bid them join us
For we travel to the ocean realm of astral kings.'
Our mind palace engages the warp drive
And we leave the hangar of anonymity for the last time.

> *The first thousand light years are the hardest,*
> *and then you enter a liquid paradise*
> *ruled by peaceful spider druids.*

`CHILDREN, PRISONERS OF MAYA!
Grow forward into your future dreams!
The backwards ego will seek its way out
whether it kills its host or not! Stop imbibing
suicide and the venom of factories! Do you
realize that everything that has ever lived
has died *except spirit?* Since this is true we
are always transitioning between two states,
but MAKE THIS STATE COUNT! Purity of
the mind is the golden nectar of God, and all
the evils and Edens you experience in this

life flavor the communal elixir of human memory. Do not ignore your heart, for it has made you what you are, and whatever journey you feel compelled to undertake, I assure you that the success of that venture rides along on your shoulder.'

D e s e r t P o e m

We gathered in the desert,
the breeze sank deep in the ravine.

Scorpions scatter clumsily over our feet.
God is in the Sun and Hell is in the thorns.

Road signs beckoned like faded postcards
leading us to this numb pilgrimage of thirst.
Vagrants bring the guns,
and we all shoot blindly into the darkness.

Deep in the mountains, inebriated bulls
charge their staggering shadows.
Vultures rend the meat off their bellies.
Crows rip their own hearts out in desperation.
This mirage has fooled everyone,
where is the feast we were promised?

We gathered in the desert,
the breeze sank deep in the ravine.

At the dinner table of lost hitchhikers
the waitress has the head of a lizard.
She brings a loaf of fury
and we all eat well.

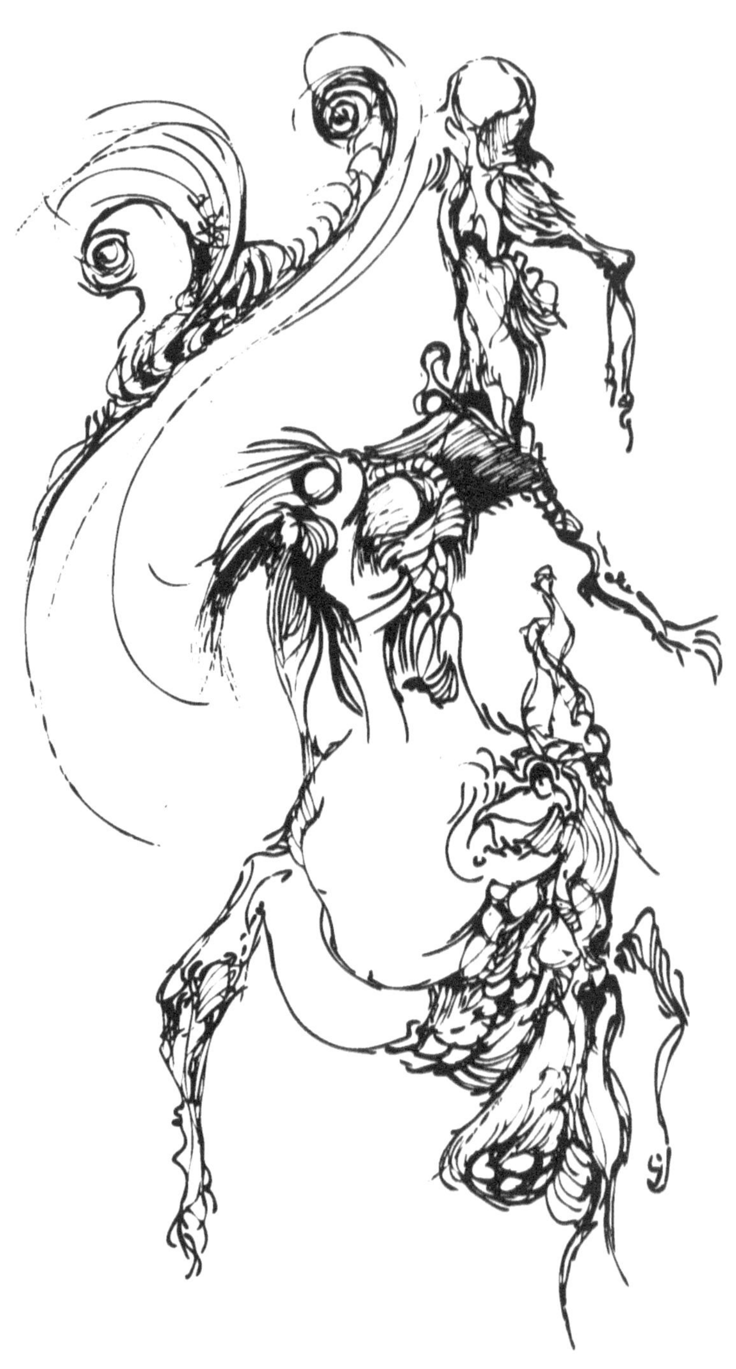

PLAGUE TRINITY
I. City Of Delirium

The milky, grey sun
birthing long shadows
in the dead dawn of industry
passes over steel stems
swaying in the city.

Bloom crowns plucked off corporate necks
thrown down in the murdering mecca
bleed the nectar of gasoline
that peasants convert to smoke.

Endless vibrating vertebrae
spawning arterial streets
crop circles of copulating GMOs
breeding in the farm of the pharaohs.

A perfect vision of imprisonment,
cameras stare down from whitewashed monuments.
Black gates keep out the masses
eating green paper, yet still they hunger,
and rush and hurry, too dizzy, too busy.

Behold, this angular forest of darkness!
Gaunt streetlights line the asphalt river
illuminating a manufactured sorrow:

A fluttering appears at the light standard.
Firing at the glowing teat
the hollow tears of wheat
whirling like nocturnal scarecrows
gasping for breath and drying in death.

And what is the cost?
One nation of moths.

II. Political Sermon

And then there were the shrieking devotees
that raced off the rails in enlightened packs.
Tripping toward the mechanical rabbit
with thundering feet, their snouts full of morals
and thinking they're sweet, they sniffed false
promises of cultural spells and melted
the metals of steely resolve.

And that old marxist arson
dribbling liberally over the kind, caring kindling
we all call humanity
erupted in flames that warmed the insane.
While degraded, serrated semen experiments
painted excrement portraits upon the cement
of post-modern cities vomiting beauty, where
wisdom and greatness were treated like vagrants.

And vain, aging sycophants decried all their duties
denying the meadow-green valleys of beauty
their fathers maintained with hard ingenuity.
Gleefully opening gates to invaders,
their hearts bled for haters with minds like grenades
while their children became new millennial slaves.

Designing sublime, shining shrines to the new
fair flesh fueled the fires that fed funeral pyres
burning all history, these blisters of idiocy
became human fuel for a burning new school.

But their children were blind, and seeking sunshine
floated without knowing up old bloody steps
hatching to birds in towers of yes, climbing
spidery skies to devise future nests.

But birds are not warriors, and as such they digressed
into floods pouring down in glittering death.

III. O v e r t u r e T o T h e B e l l y O f A S w a n

Galloping, buzzing horseflies
charge riderless into battle
a fray of infestation
in the failing light of a total eclipse.

Dogfight dragonflies
insects of arson
fill foe with flame
while the dropping dead make locust rain
and the moths tend the wounded butterflies
in the burn ward.

zzzZZZZZZZZZ
Wasps in their black shirts
with segmented engine husks
mimic black and yellow torpedoes
dropping on an unsuspecting populace.
And devouring walls of aphids
bank hard in the sudden spotted sunset,
a phalanx of ladybugs.

This mad, humming warfare
of blinding herds obscure the stars,
like tiny propellers of the apocalypse
creating a permanent midnight.

Fireflies flicker and spark in the dark
lighting the Allied onslaught.

Hellfire hornets
  battle the bluebottles
    diving stings

       whirling wings
     a furious fog
   of seething skins
     bleeding bombs of buzz
       sawing wings of fuzz
         hovering high over
           the hazy horizon.
             Maddening motors, moaning drones
               multiplying into meals
                 f   o
                  o   f
                    r   d
                      t   e
                        h   v
                          e   o
                        h   u
                      o   r
                        r   i
                          r   n
                            i   g
                              f   s
                                i   w
                                  c   a
                                    d   n
                                      r   s
                                        e
                                      a
                                    m

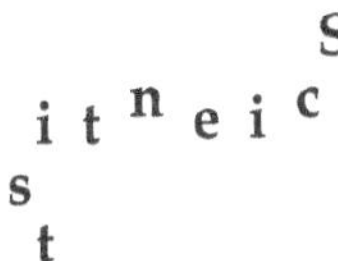

I'm building a bomb of birds.
I've mounted round rows of claws so my
bird bomb can climb mountain cities. Brain
mounted to the top, pointing north. Eyes seeking
the way, bulging brilliantly from iron cheeks, little
squinting target sensors on-high. The flattened skull
forms a thin coating on my bomb secreting it passed
any radar. Bird fat applied quite sparingly over the
bomb reduces friction. The heart hangs from
a long, slim ribbon far below, leading
children to the detonation.

Frontline Snapshot

When God built me for your visual pleasure
he used hunger to make my bones
sighs for my breasts
sparrows whirring in the birdcage of my heart
flickering eyelids for hiding dread
and a pretty swan neck for propping up screams.

I AM THE BRITTLE BRIDE OF MATCHSTICKS
    a daring red boat
    a flirtatious fountain of blood
dashing through the masculine imagination of war.

  I am caught -
    in your
    obscene
    immortal
      stare.

[And the billboard in the center of town
        is massive and invisible]

45

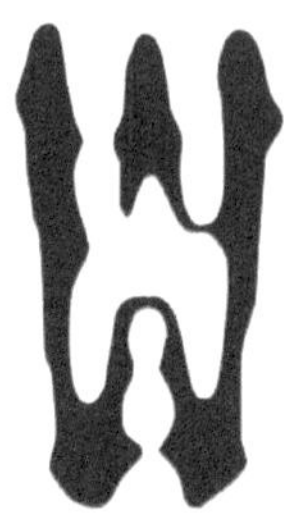
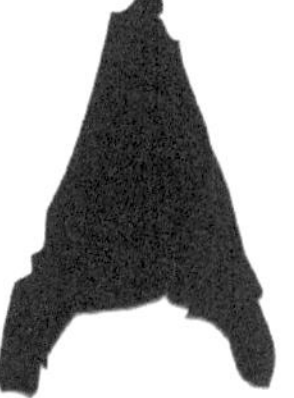
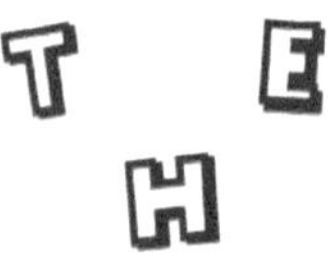

W

A

R

EAT$

THE

poor

Tyrant

Tyrant, little tyrant
Beady-eyed dominator
Pestilential pretender
Nothing Man with a gut of flies.

The applause is recorded
Your admirers are all dead
How do the marionette strings feel
Cutting into your shoulders?

Tyrant, little tyrant
Do you mistake your jerking movements for free will?
No time to stop now, little rabbit
There are more people to kill.

Genocide Water Fountain

Long ago, in the land of the unending dole, some bellies were filled `til they fell to the floor. Bursting in gluttony, a fine flooding felony trickling down to ravenous peasants milling around, and seeing the trickle they fell to the ground! Dammed the deluge, slurped up the crude, chewing the feuds `til their tongues became fused. And once they were sated the peasants decided a motion to honor the potion be made, exhaling the oceans the bellies once craved. So a fountain projecting the festering gore was founded for young mining mouths to explore, a bright shining beacon of watery reason provided to hordes who would come to the fore, proclaiming the wisdom of cannibal ore! And so, on it went, that greedy young peasants gave up their dissent, arriving in millions to drink at the fountain the townsfolk invented with every slurp spent.

And this was the birth of government.

A m e r i c a n s

We blow the brass bugle of independence
Breathing steam locomotive dreams
Riding the triumphant stallion of ideas
Nothing and no one will tame us
The modern world is the flower of our minds
And we will not be evicted!

Pilgrims by the millions become holy mages
Turn away from chattering birds made of cages
Our faces carved from the stone of the ages
The conquering kind evolves and rewinds
Refines the mass mind and seeks absolution
Forging heaven is the new revolution!

Once we were cannibals, now we're magicians.
Invasions to inventions, vengeance to friendships.

Attaining the summit, we step into wind
Striding the air with our forefather's care
The dare of a nation, reborn and divine
We are the infants of time.

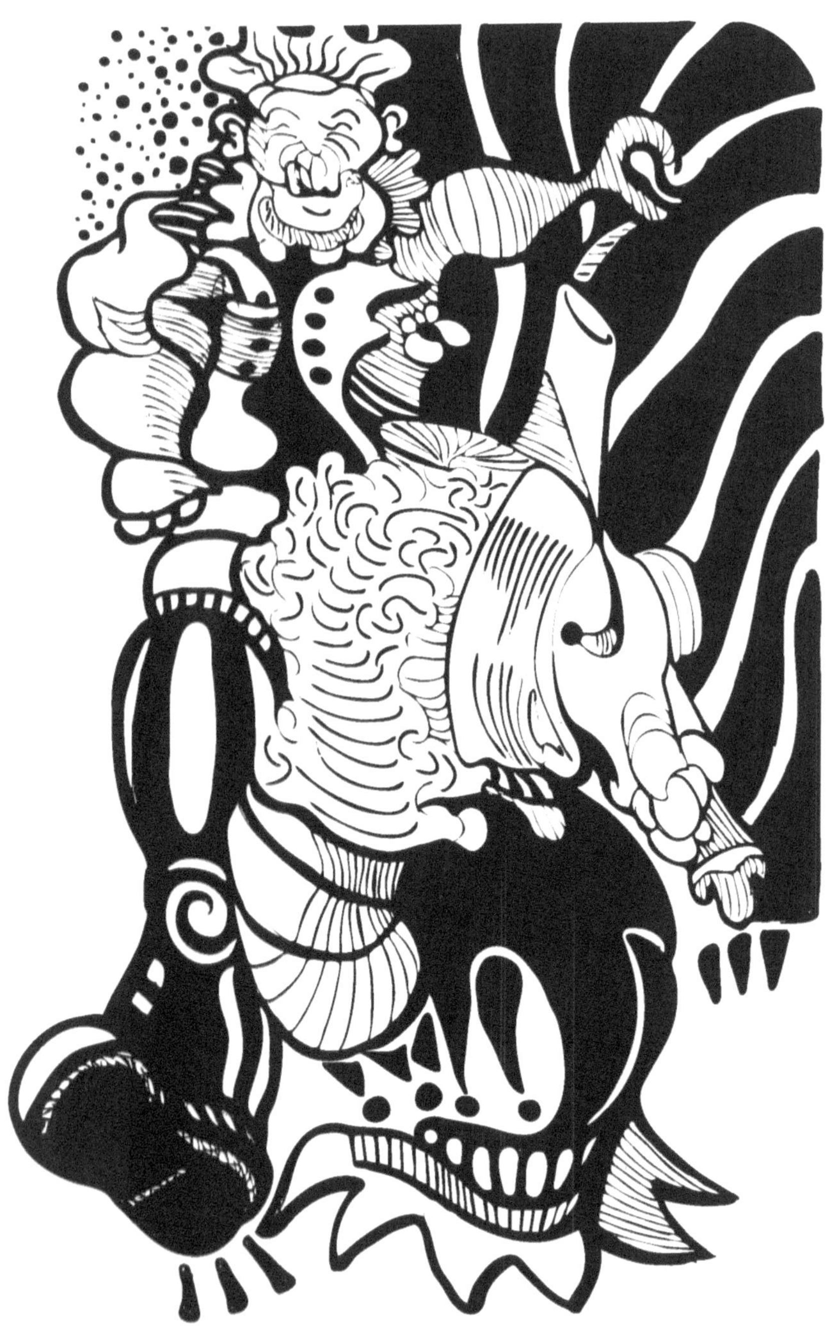

A Barrage of Firework Poems in Celebration of the Poet's Birthday

Welcome to a world of infinite possibilities! I will be your host and guide. The distorted crown of reverence rests on your head as we greet the flaming orb of abundance. Its tail of sparking rainbows will alleviate any and all malignant curses, joints, rheumatisms, et al. Look into my bag of artifacts! The first item is the ointment of Eros, a pinkish healing salve made of morning glories mixed with only the finest butter. The second is the Staff of Water, a crystal of such divine and elusive lights that it shames the most brilliant of maniacal jellyfish. Immerse it in your sink and rain will drench your garden. The third is the root from the Brigtarllyg Tree, a mythical tower seven leagues high that existed before rats invaded the blue temples of Io. If rotated in the eye of a hurricane, terrible calamities will be visited upon your enemies. The fifth is the heart of a cloud doe. Rubbed on the lips of a woman, she will soon experience erotic animal fantasies tearing through her body in feverish paroxysms. Use sparingly. The sixth is the sap of the tar fruit stored in the skull of an elephant's first born male. Rub this into your ribcage and you will fly effortlessly! For this treasure trove, I ask only for seven rubies and for your pilgrimage to the grave of Rimbaud. There you will meet Lachlan, Keeper of Souls, who will ask for all the memories of your childhood.

*

I am the weaver of winds
the mythical cloud giant
I stand six miles high
the flesh of my body
contains within it
worlds of fantastic design
my fingernails
horde the sands
of ancient deserts
my teeth are blue scarabs
I will melt into the Earth
and peace and joy
will reign forever.

*

Tree green tree blue
leaf black leaf yellow
rain red rain white
stars
stones
stalactites
tunneling mole
cave of runes
acorn meat
drink of dew
tunneling mole
scallion moons
lichen sweet
granite flue
tunneling mole
cracked quartz
radish shoots

moldering foal
tunneling mole
t
  u
    n
  n
e
  l
    s
      d
     o
  w
n
    its
hole in the
   g
   r
   o
   u
   n
   d
(cathedral of snails).

*

Delicate eel with the dagger grin,
your forked tail twitches under the

unblinking eye of a young woman
watching one note of music cut from

glass, reach the smoky ceiling and shatter.
When the unrepentant tenants run in the room

one story up, I think of ten thousand
murders and the riot race of idiots

born to derail my steamenginedoubloons
cascading in rivulets around the cape of

ink to the broad beach of anvils. Maybe,
dear eel, you can practice the Egyptian

technique of brain removal on these whomans
until only their hate keeps them alive.

*

It's not the older-getting
but the death-bedding closeness
of the clock hand grabbing you
roughly by the collar screaming
exhortations of wasted afternoons
and tasted macaroons, until the golden
imagination stream has milked the last
glacier of gems, leaving only the most
meager of milky opals tippling
off your failing fingertips
and sounding crooked notes
on a detuned piano.

But wait,
no, the imagination is a muscle!
Cousin of latissimus dorsi,
dorsal fin of creation liners,
powering though the heady rapids
of a volatile youth
to a pineapple paradise
melting on the distant horizon

visible from the corner
of your once-dormant eye.

*

Maid of anesthesia
thine eyes are to me like
2 bowls of banyan leaves
forming the beds
of yawning Margay cats.

Let's climb the ravaged peaks
of each other's patience
and force every human emotion
into a tear, deep enough to drown
the California Penal System.

*

`Attention-La boisson que vous allez
savourer est extremement chaude!'*

The poem that will scald your tongue
when drunk aloud is the distillation
of many years of Armageddon uncertainties
chandeliers of crystalline insults
candle flames in dark brothels
the boiling soup of Macbeth's
witch-chorus of expositions.

It eats like acid
smothers like wax
its very vowels groan
from the mouth of Charon

uttering your penance for the
ride across the river Styx.

Not even Dante can save you now,
you've already read too far.
Creeping passed orchards of heads
sprouting like potatoes from their graves.

You feel a slight itching trouble
your spine, this is the poison
poem doing its foul work.
Drop the book and flee the
coffee shop, it will do you no good.
Your last will and testament
is a white butterfly fluttering just
beyond your dying grasp.

I'm sorry for what I had to do to you
but it was necessary.

*   *   *

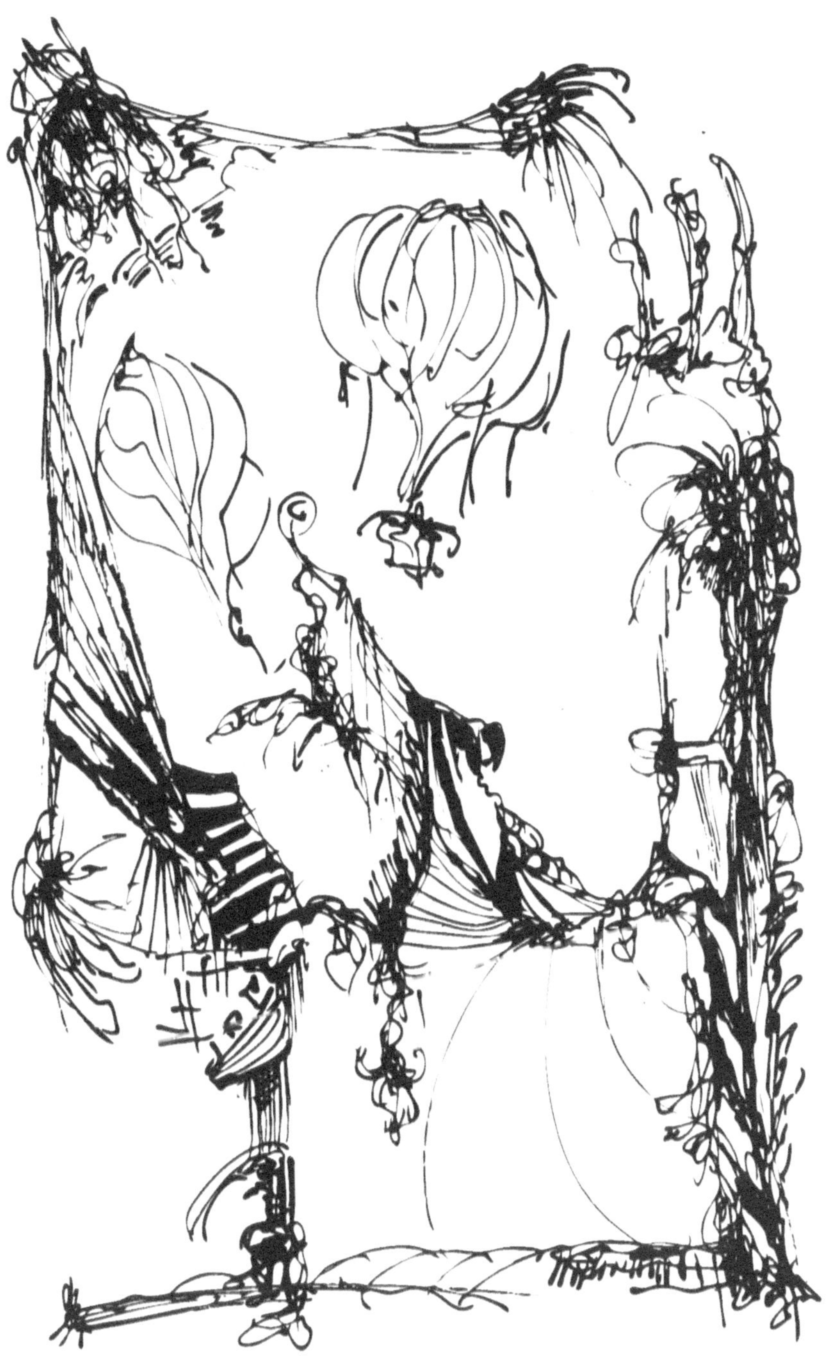

I Am A Bar
(A Toast For Those About To Drink)

And all of the cocktails I've ever imbibed
Fill up this drunken man made of hide.
It's my body, hot toddy, rum, whisky and wine
Tequila that spills from my ears through the years
And not one of my family abstains, in their veins
Run liquors of magical, wondrous designs.

Their cheeks are like apples, rosy and kind
Dropping from branches heavy with vines
But when *my* time comes, my blood will become
The new alcohol, the punch of the ball,
Unavailable at even the finest rum halls.

So tap these veins and extract the fine essences
Shaming all artful, aged and blessed vintages
The warmest burnt bourbons, the twang of mescals
These liquors will make you and me such great pals!

And that's not all, Willy Wonka would fall
To his knees at the staggering, rainbow varieties
Churning in tidal waves, bubbling in pools
Of drooling green oranges, violets and blues
My liver will ooze such cerulean juices
My kidneys impart woozy brews to peruse!

A mind-altering buzz, my blood is manna!
Swirling humanity drunk with abandon
Brandies and blood cells fighting off boredom
Oh Lord, it's these fickle and inhumane times
Making one pickle their parts with all kinds
But my vintage is prime! And comets alight to ignite

My blood whisky, so let's all get frisky and tap this aorta
I taste most like caramel plums, kinda sorta.

    Cauldrons of coffee steeped in scotch brine
    Tapping my grappa heart pumping out wine.

There's a lot that can be got
And it sure don't cost a lot
But don't go dredging my keg for the dregs
The finest is spooned from the top!

Sunset

100 year-old pelican
skimming across the mirroring sea
clouds high above follow the crawling crabs
giant shells of darkness creeping over the sand
the tides and the sleek, twisting animals spearing the waves
mist pirouettes in the white surf
the sun painting the sea orange
dying into the horizon like
a yellow actress.

Cinematic Women

   Dancers are mad spinning tops teetering
on the edge of wooden cliffs, blood-rushing
sacrificial marionettes, hypnotic birds
   flying into themselves.

   Black & white Marlene Dietrich dolphin
in a satin waterfall, sunhair sensual angel.

   There is a movie trapped in her body
& midnight rolls in ringlets around her shoulders.
She swallowed an hourglass when she was young
and now she has the body of a woman
   and the arms of zebras.

   She is the volcano and the aftermath
dark explosion ocean with blood sand.
   China doll siren in a red torture chamber.

   She stared at a cat too long when she was a girl
and it gave her those lovely eyes.
   Her body is made of mountains and rivers
and her heart is a clock full of honey.

The Bride Of Webs

Silken strands
criss-cross my pale skin.
'Lie still', the bride commands,
and her spinning, delicate touch
wraps my bursting body harvest.

Fertile arachnid
teetering over her canyon of webs
reflecting the sky with a thousand black eyes
her cries dripping acid, her flickering visage
lovely and placid, her craft commanding
a bountiful orchard, binding the fly
in sweet torture.

My alabaster creeping queen
  your prison embrace
  your poison kiss
I shudder in white cocoons,
soft as an echo's breath
in the red kingdom of spiders.

Endless Maidens With Very Long Eyes

Wizard licker
Agate eyed
Acid crystal
Jester jawed
Snake finger
Siren crier
Ocean mouth
Spider clever
Rabbit touching
Blood running
Star gazer
Night creeper
Mind hummer
Merry maker
Time walker
Levitator
Cello hips
Mellow lips
Breast hills
Lace thrills
Bucking mare
Chaos diver
Silence wearing
Ever caring
Childbearing
Hypnotizer.

Storm drinker, spitting fire
pretty pyre, walking wires
wanting all, wrecked and sad
always crooked, wicked, bad
madly made in Sappho's cave

born of waves, carved in jade
lying in the mushroom shade.

My whole life I've been searching
for endless maidens
   with
   very
   long
   eyes.

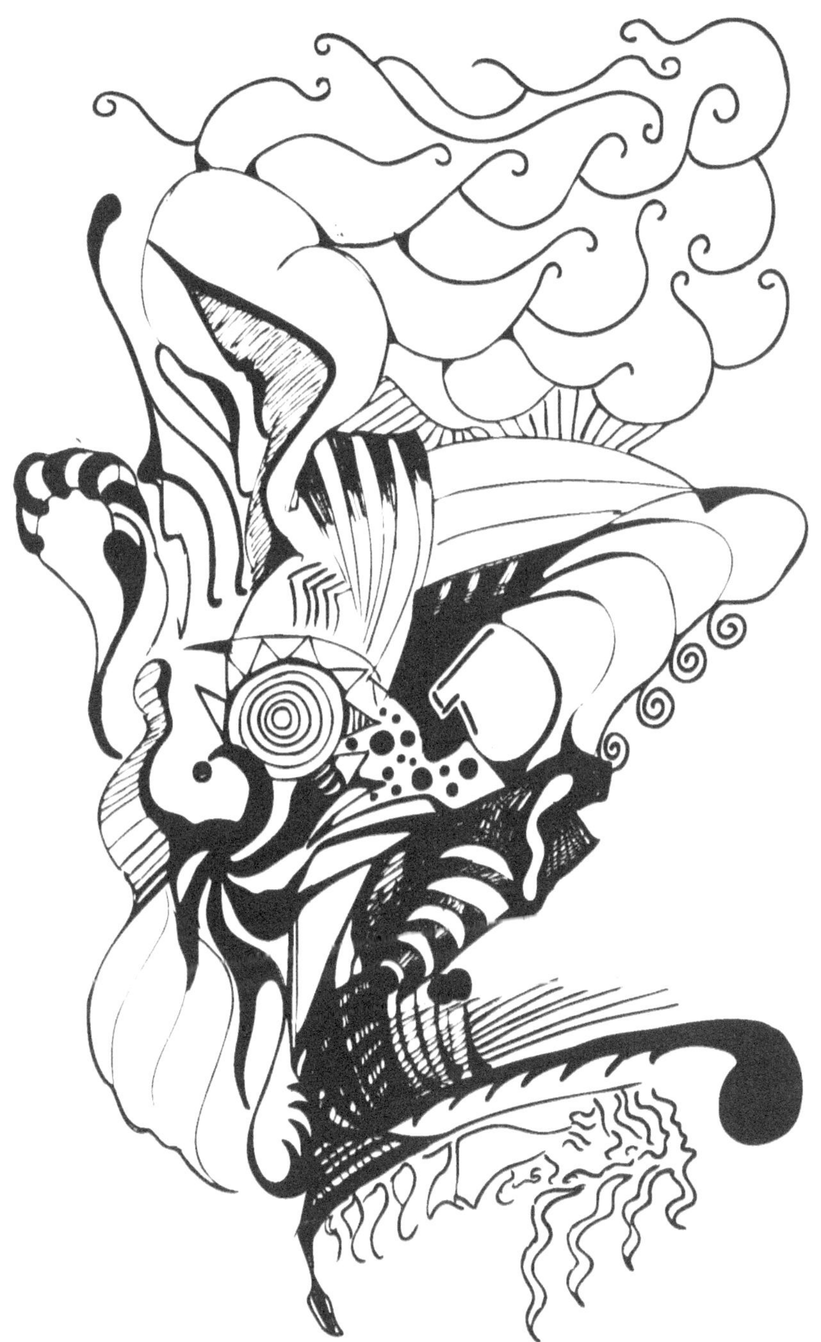

I Don't Want A Woman Who's Not Like The Sun

I don't want a woman who's not like the sun,
a pin-up poster without any tongue
an arrogant one, an unloaded gun
stiletto fellatio without any passion
a mannequin simply existing for fashion
a carbon-copy of a bygone age
a kite that blows across the stage
a doll in a box that's never been touched
a princess performing for a bitter man's lust
a sickly-sweet cocktail without any alcohol
a priestess who'll never evolve, not at all
an elegant prop for a crumbling marriage
a horseless carriage parading through Paris
a motionless mop of hair in my bed
a basket of bones that cannot be bled
a volcano that's dormant with nary a torrent
a directionless leaf blowing west and then east
expecting the world to appease her at least
as she teases her hair, but I can't even stare
at a girl who hasn't a clue, so I'm blue
for not one of these, one of these
women are true, they weep
and they rue, but
I only want
you.

Ruins

In the city of strange laughing faces
black thoughts infect the flesh
turn blood to ash.

The ceiling watches the insects below
walled-in ordered lives.
The floor props them up, shrieking statues
frozen silent in crooked tasks.

Here comes the beautiful infestation!
The rusted armor scales
crack like crustaceans
and rays of honey
rain in the rooms
from above.
It is LOVE.

An Inventory of A Servant's Pockets At The Time Of His Death

-for Arthur Conan Doyle

There was a box of vestas,
two inches of tallow candle,
an A.D.P. briar-root pipe,
a pouch of sealskin with half an ounce
of long-cut Cavendish,
a silver watch with a gold chain,
five sovereigns in gold,
an aluminum pencil-case,
a few papers,
and an ivory-handled knife
       with a very delicate
              inflexible blade
marked Weiss & Co.,
London.

Sonnet Of Small Woe
-for the unknown, abused son

mom, she had a boy, shedidntmeanto.
a crying thing made of blubber and blood
and young joy. all afraid he was, and blue
from the grabbing and greedy hands that brood

around beer cans late at night conducting
aluminum music. not like the songs
of her dancing days, mind you. girls twisting
in petal dresses under boys of strong

desire. in the back of the car they ate
temtation's fruit. but shedidntmeanto.
i was the little seed he spit, too late
to fix, providing a body well-bruised

that stops the hand in swinging. i rattle
like a cup of shells that never mattered.

The Manifesto Has Gotten Into
The Transformer!
-for Anthony Frewin

Like Kafka's castle,
their inhumane decrees perplex, act defiant, and
multiply in hateful omnipotence at a climber's height.
Dr. Moreau has taken over as head breeder due to falling
birth rates from endless entertaining distractions, aerial
chemical castration, and sheer overwhelming
materialism.

And in the worker-slums, the ape-men
are carrying hammers and the gentle rat-children
elicit our sympathy.

The prisoner, Frank R. Paul, recording great moments in
the pornography of violence, impatiently awaits the
arrival of Flash Gordon. On his feet are small turbines,
compressing the air beneath him as he succeeds in
melting the bars of his prison and fleeing a trio of
frightening automatons. He switches off the turbines
and rests in the curve of a cave wall under the vast
towering columns that arise from the depths of the Earth,
dwarfing the subterraneans.

And far below, the Princes of A. I. drink espresso
in the cafes, prop their metal feet on the corpses of the
proletariat, and declare their manifestoes with high-
pitched squeals of murderous machine sound.

Frank turns his face from the exploding sky, rolls his
own scroll of manifestoes tightly and slides it
underneath his arm. He knows now that Flash will
never come. He is unaware that Flash has his own

problems, near death he is, on another plane and under a searing second Sun, battling gallantly with Aparo, the Lunarian leader.

Once a functionary of the Engineering Guild
Aparo gifted himself to Dr. Moreau to further his career
and now his tentacles flail in fury as he wars
with Flash in unholy anger.

Aparo, wielding a six-sided crystal made from the eyes of Horus, succeeds in capturing Flash in a vortex of colors, shooting him imprecisely through time. Aparo understands that the Princes of A.I. clearly dislike this man, and he wanted to further their clockwork agenda with his remaining life force. After vanquishing Flash and fulfilling his purpose, he waves to the Lunarians and recedes into the twilight world of the rooftops, remembered only as a step on the stairway of the Princes' evil, metallic dreams.

Flash lands in a heap in 1844, his memory forgotten,
his body broken and scarred. He becomes a salesman
of laughing gas for the physically-exhausted incubator
and rents a 1-bedroom flat from a landlord he despises.

Back in 2065, the citizens no longer work, or sleep, or dream, or hope, and spend their days submitting to machines, receiving vibratory-induced debilitations and daily injections of radium isotopes. But in a divine twist of fate, Frank discovers the demolition sequence that was born within the design of the Engineering Guild, and he triggers it, emerging triumphantly from its smoking wreckage. Standing high on its crushed cement turrets, he grasps the bronze aerial switch of the Machine Of

Possibility and turns it clockwise, causing the societal engineers in the mammoth transmitter tube to disappear.

He has finally realized he is his *own* hero,
and has stepped into pure destiny
like a fine, crystalline waterfall
becoming imagination.

The pure humans that remained began ignoring the insane whims of authority and started having beautiful human children again, while the micro chipped, self-hating cyborgs rotted in sad, transhuman degradation in their seething slums of singularity, and the day finally came when the Princes of A.I. were vanquished forever, not by man's belligerent technologies, but by bacteria.

Mad Machines

Ingest or arrest this fiend of distress.
The crabs crawl sideways in crooked dances over blank expressions and the Sun steals glances into dusty windows revealing sorrows. Why do we work so hard, why do we sulk so hard, there is a light at the end of the turbine grinding out tin pan alley from an archonic phonograph cackling with witches spitting poisons in our potions pushing our heads in a caduceus noose shooting the skies dead with white webs slaking the thirst from the man-eating hearse while slithering snakes slide through the doors of the doll house and the doll house is burning the doll house is burning our fear only feeding the flames in their fury taking our lashes as aftermath ashes nursing red shocks and wasting our water on whiskies and rocks while history screams from a forest of clocks, where can we find a fireman in flames, we'll never be heroes when we're always waiting to be saved.

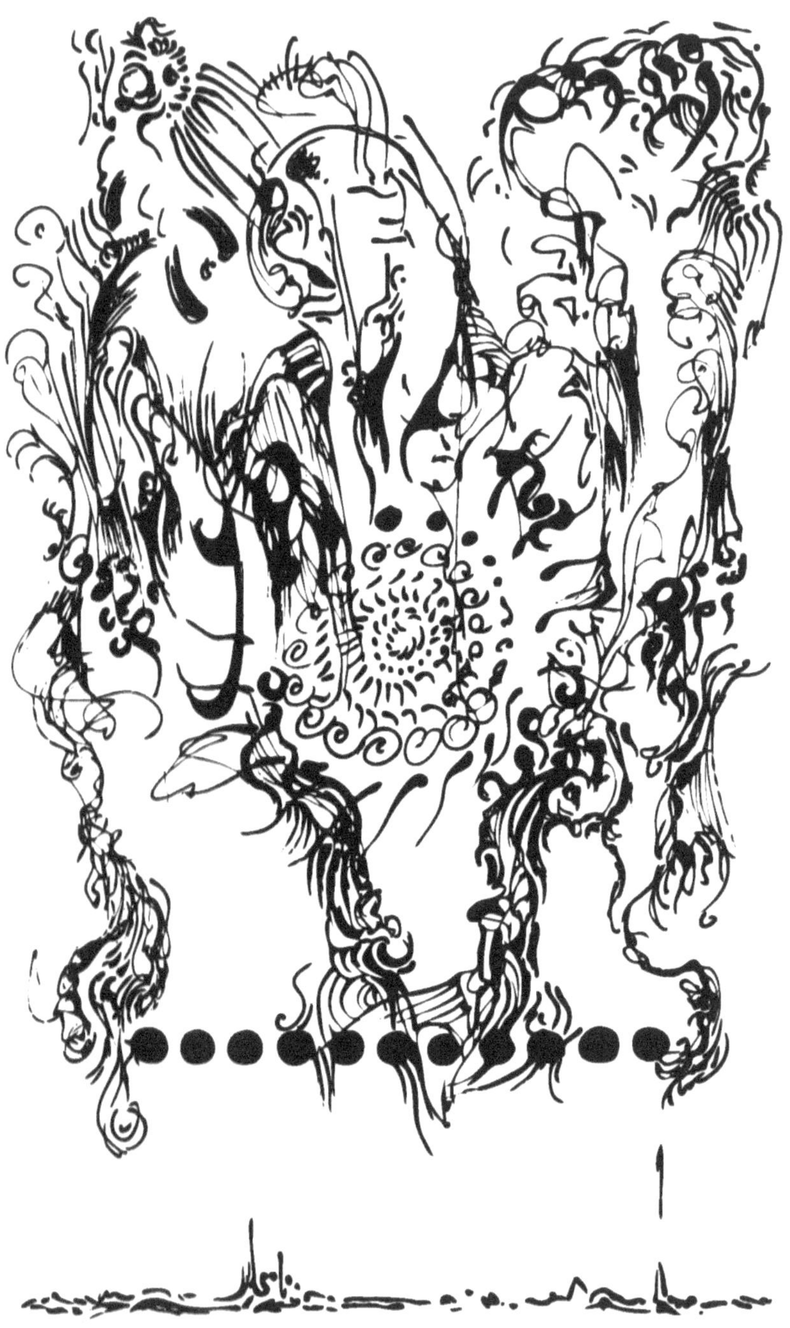

Body Freedom

Your body is a traveling renaissance fair of carnal pleasure, a key made of flesh that opens the little gates of heaven. So explore the arenas of desire if you dare, sinful boudoirs disobeying decency, vehicular motels overlooking the city, or the endless, expansive caravan of procreation that created us all. But while you are free, my friend, to recite the monologue of the libertine, know that the Universe loves you more when you love another, you will be anointed with euphoria and your wife will help carry your soul into heaven, for civilization is a crib made of branches for lonely souls, touching each other's fingertips and breathing like the crashing ocean.

Danger

ART

conformity

---safety---

Civilization Vs. Bird Song

There is a whistling and the birds shut off. Swirling esses escaping a teapot, a teapot brimming with hisses and screams, sugar and cream. The whistling hissing persists in perniciously silencing avian keening.

> *Slithering sounds nest-bound*
> *break the bells of bird song.*

There is a squawk of metal talk and the birds shut off. Morning engines cough at attention, jittery hawks erupt in mad flocks, fleeing the coughing cacophonous shock. Flickery, trickery beaks switch off at the metal talk squawk.

> *shhhhhhhhh*

At noon, the coughing house coughs loud. Shingled land whale wailing anguish, slamming panic, brandishing ambush.

Nest birds shush in a willow, normally mellow and willing in filling the willow with pillowy songs, the poor feathered throngs prolonged in awe, deny their high-flying tunes, and soon they're swooning in non-crooning gloom, portending the ending of singing at noon.

The nest birds shush and herd their words with courteous vows, with the silence of clouds, the avian crowd is no longer aloud (in truth, they just think they're no longer allowed), as the proud and coughing house coughs loud.

Doggies braying, loudly growling, braying with their snouting open wide with flailing tongues assailing songs outside.   The doggie's flogging tongue is flailing, howling from its snouting wailing wild and open wide, the other side of its tail outside.   Doggies braying, growling daily, shunning song, declaring hunger, every howl creating thunder, the huffing, harking, following thunder ripping the birdsong asunder.

The very air is endless cacophony,
nest of hushing necessarily.

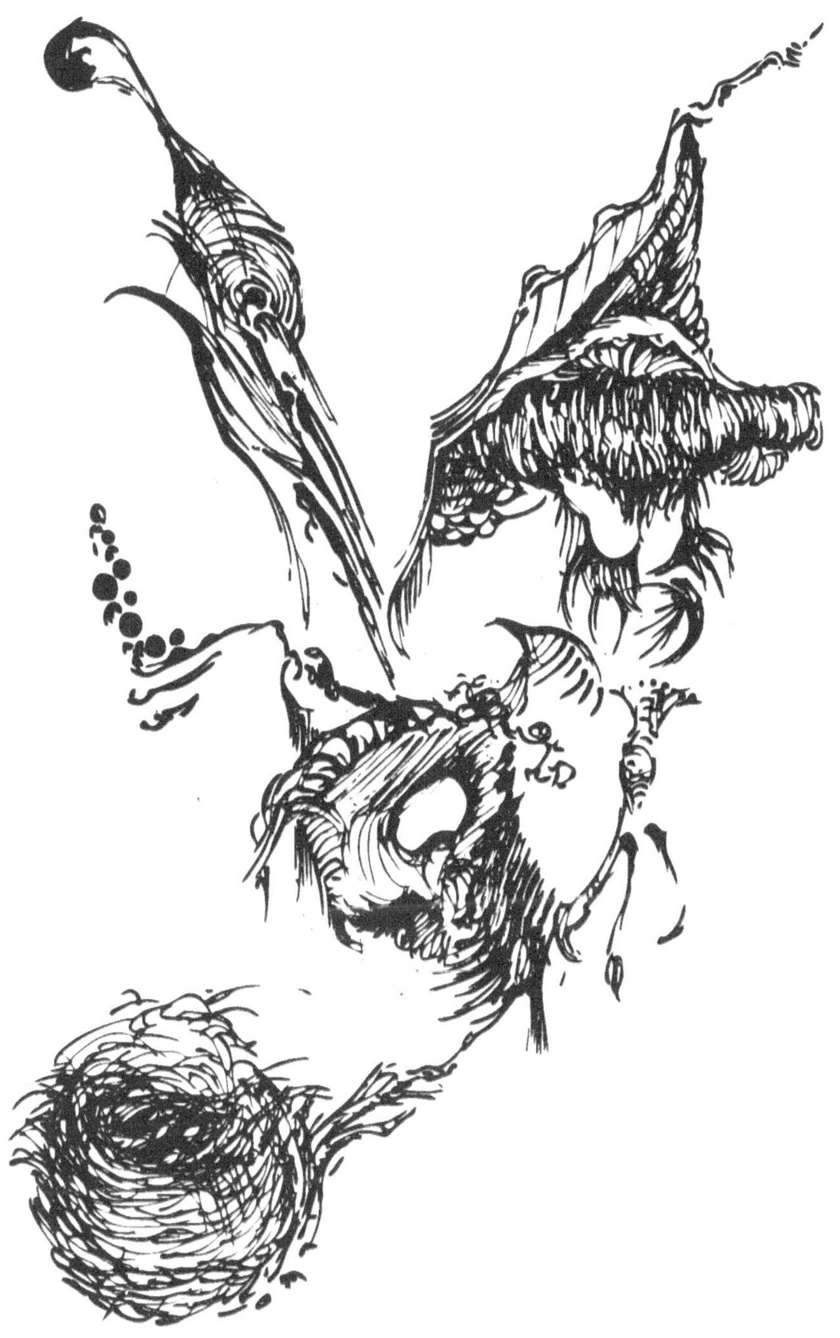

Mermaid Of The Fog

Pour yourself a highball, this one'll take a while.

My grandma was a grass skirt swaying Southern Belle
daughter, living life lover, five child mother, chef like
no other, jingle singer center stage, sipped that bourbon
Ancient Age, never flew into a rage, kept our hearts in
a granny cage, drank like a man and drove by the sand.
(In a Volkswagen Bug, not a smooth sedan).

> Never changed from the 50's
> Sheltered the rain of the 60's
> Hosted bevies of revelries in the heavy 70's
> And was always a lady, well in her 80's.

I'd make the long drive up from LA to fry calamari in
her well-kept beach nest. Watched the stage plays of her
actor son, read the pirate tales of her sailor son, and
heard sweet harmonies from her three girls in curls.
(One raised me from a babe like a mad oyster pearl).

> Even before I could drink I was high
> with heady glee, rocking in the rocking chair,
> `ol granny and me.

Her favorite album was *Stardust* by Willie Nelson.
Though partial she was to Gabby Pahinui and the
drunken guitars of Hawaii. And it was there she met
her man, a handsome baseball player, sherry drinker.
Liked his booze in a yellow tin cup, ogled all the ladies
but never gave her up, lorded at the home but never said
much. (He mostly sat still while the children ran ragged
`round his old sofa chair in the living room wagon).

But ladies first, and his ample thirst was sated by that
gold-plated gal that God created. She was sane through
clouds of mary jane when The Beatles reigned, and
never tittered an ill-word to others (though maybe Glen
Miller was her druthers).

Her home was an old-time steamship of memories
and my prose lies down at her feet without vanity.

In my life I've observed much but said little.
She seemed to understand the brasswork ticking
~ of my childhood mind ~
that effervescent knowingness unnoticed by time.

Later in life, on nights when I wore the New England
jacket of a writer, we lit crackling infernos in her brick
fireplace. There never was a cinder that jumped to the
shag, and burned us alive like a mad, fiery hag. We
were ill-equipped for a Dalmation-level inferno, but no
dangers ever crept in her palace of drafts, and the
morning was coffee and big belly laughs.

We were safer then when people
thought less and felt more.

Shaking powdered chicken in a brown paper bag,
breaking the brittle tips of green beans in her hands,
(was this necessary in the land of cans?)

She was queen of the kitchen and lady of the manor.
And when the howl of family drama hurled its insults
like snow drifts at her foggy porch, they were met only
with love, laughter and flickering firelight.

There were no searing knives that failed
to turn to butter in her portly paws.

Some days I crept with trepidation down her
dirtfloorcellardungeon of one-red-dot black widow
spiders. The awkward jutting sofa and depression-era
bicycle; a museum of darkness it was. But the backyard
cellar was always peculiar. No one ever ventured there,
ignored at the family events like the mutant stepchild of
some 70's horror flick.

The night before she died
I drove 400 miles to hold her hand.

That wonderful, laughing, bit player from a Dickens
novel who drank bourbon like a whale swallows
seawater, lounging in her pink terrycloth jumpsuit,
watching "Are You Being Served" on an ancient box
of rickety images.

One day her neighbors complained about the foghorn
down by the light house. They argued it was
unnecessary in this age of nautical certainty.
They shut it off, and there were only waves.

But that foghorn was like you, Grandma.
Antique and shining, dispensing sanity and direction
in a petty, trifling world. You each were extinguished
by the mad march of time, never to be seen in this world
again.

Once you were gone, your old, creaky beach house
was sold off its wooden stilts and replaced by a cold

and modern oasis of convenience. I toured that undead
house one day,

I wish I hadn't.

S p i n e s
-for Mom

Cantankerous beasties, starving beauty.
See the seething beasties
begging, biting, craving
meaty treats
from meaty feasties.
Trumpeting toadies
croak below the
wicked witches toasting tails
simmering saucy
snakes & snails
cauldron bubbling
tempting beasties
up the hungry hills and dells.
Beasty gypsies
tripping tipsy
hide the hills in hordes
hear the bells of toads
mad galumphing
hungry tummies
up the hungry hills and dells.
Clawing shores, the beasties shiver
climbing cauldrons, seeking supper
falling in with simmering kin,
bubbling up with
struggling litters
of feisty, feasty
stewing critters,
the witch sits
down to
dinner.

Do You Know Where
The Blue Fairy Lives?

They will take me to the flesh fair
        where dreams meet death
                and b-l-o-o-d
                        is slavery.
d i s c a r d e d toys
                                are bright
                                a n d
                                w-r-h-e-s
                                o-t-l-s
        teddy bears hug and
                    kiss memory.
            i can work
        don't you worry
            i'll take you
            i'll take you
        to pretty rouge city
                i'll get
            you your
            c o f f e e
                    m
                    a
                    s
                    s
                    a
                    g
                    e
                your
            fair   feet
        don't believe in the lies
        of my kind, i am kind
            and i'll barter
        the street with nine lives

that don't matter
			like batteries made
from battered wives making batter.

	don't burn me please, sir
i'm not pinocchio the toy, i'm a boy.
	&
	   w
	     o
		o
		  d
		    e
		      n
			children
			s
			p
			i
			l
			l
milk ever after
  but never *my* kind
	we're clever forever.
		mad wanderers we, we're b r o k e n
  but hoping over hey kitty kitty
		are you her
		  oh, she's pretty
the lady
	of	im
		ma
		culate hearts
		is another
& dr. know knows where everyone goes
his advice is combined with every tale told.

`come away
little mecha
to the end of the world'

where dreams will weep
into oceans that call me.
i'm no canary
i won't tell
your secrets, so keep me
please keep me
i suffer mistakes
they made when they made me.

and
when all
blood dries
architectural texture
the landlord leaves for
a heavenly lecture, but i am
immortal, i'll stay by your side
tethered to flesh that calls itself mother.
please read me, please sit me
i'll be friends
with
the *other*
i'm david
i'm david
i'll be his real brother.

`What a success you've become, well
done little child!   Chasing your
dreams no machine has compiled,
we thank you, we spank you, we
bank you in droves, the mothers
who dive into futures want children

created in technical joy, for you are
the truest flesh carved in a toy. But
cities underwater will bring you no
angels, so please David please,
believe in our joy, in a cage, in a
cage, through a door we wage war,
every door like a sore will open in
rage, so please act your age and love
every dream, they made you you
know, a foe to our foe, a toy for a lie,
i must say goodbye, but please go in
joy, please be a real boy.'

mommy, you threw me away.
      or at daddy's request,
   doesn't matter i guess.
            time is a gift
                        for
                        no
                           one
            who's left.
      but now
      time
      belongs to
whoever can
      bless me 'cuz
   time ate my years and
                     fear
                  ate
                  the
            rest.
are you my mother?
are you my mother?
      there is no other
and even I give her

            my heart
          o my he*art*
i'm a l-o-s-e-r, for
                    e

                  v

                e

              r
i love her but soon
                        l o s e
                           my
                         grip
when the *other* comes
my fingers fall dead and i
                              l

                         o

               s

         e
her
i
lose
her
            she's g o n e now
        f

          o

            r

              e

                v

                  e

                    r
she's gone for an*other*
      so high and so smiling
               so h
                     i
                    g
                  h

and so softly
she left me in high
g - *u* - *s* - *t* - *s*
                    of
                              w
                              i
                         n
                      d and I'm sorry, so
h
i
g
h
and so
l
o
v
e
l
y
goodnight and goodbye,
          I'll find
   a
     n
   o
     t
   h
     e
   r
       who'll love me, she'll
            love me but

w h y ?

Poem For Jim Morrison

Let the incantation begin,

Jim, Venice is dying.
The tongue of the speculator licks down the marrow.
The soul of the city suffocates in
  the sticky saliva of its corporate kiss.
Rats march down Abbot Kinney
  with paint cans strapped to their spines
  scurrying to the rhythms of consumerism.

Long gone is the oxygen kiss of jazz horns
  the acid-fueled sunshine, the God-throb of ideas
  the rule of love, the white knights of imagination
  lighting fires with a burning piano.

Now, palm trees lean at the sun
  like teetering matchsticks.
This once village of cobras is bloodless
  and the fangs crumble in your hands.

But still some mercurial serpent
stalks the beaches at night,
and the waves, the waves,
crashing into the cymbals of the surf.

We're all lost on the highway, Jim.
        Searching for the crystal ship.
    I see my name etched in granite
        but the monument is virginal white
not some surrealist headstone
        buried in flowers at the Père Lachaise
    or scrawled in a jukebox of old legends
        rusting in sawdust at Hinano's Café.

I've seen men claw illusions in masks of loneliness
I've seen the women, carnivalesque, daring, aching
I've watched the crooked and tribal Hollywood dreams
 the blood ocean battlefields blinding all morality
 veterans eaten raw by your false flag father
 lemonade children seeking God in a rhyming television
 migrant souls burning in brushfires.

I drank whisky in the roadhouse
  kissed the woman, Los Angeles.
But today troubadours are shot on sight.
They're living in the fear of possibility.
They're calling to you, Oak Man!
Your seeds have taken root
   but you'll never meet your children,
   savage, beautiful, writhing in young lust
   and rebellion. Pretty, soft insects
   with eyes like smoldering suns.

They laid him in the ground as the shaman spoke,
        he railed at the frost in the winter of zombies
        his breath caught fire and became summer
        his cries ripped a hole in heaven
        letting in the wandering vagabonds
        his blood grew mysterious red flowers
        in Death's lonely garden.

Fly Jim, fly!
The Lords are at your heels!
Leap from your grave before they uproot you
  and call it a harvest!

Play It Again, Syd

Syd Barrett,
orchestral diamond cutter
finger painting the Union Jack
he died twice, once in the spotlight
twice as a Cambridge time gardener.

The clown prince of the London underground
wrote tales of gnomes in the acid-drenched forest.
The peculiar leaf that tried to steal the tree
Lucifer Sam selling astronomy.

Emily drinks from a garden hose
spies that old jack rabbit legend in waistcoat
from the corner of her sunlit eye
down the dark hole of an English meadow he goes
chemical animal in top hat and monocle
original, virginal sifting through sands,
Emily tries, but misunderstands.

Lighters flicker in the smoky sound
airplanes dive in the dance club
sinister songs from strings and fair fingers
a careening, melodic madness unfurls
swirling in colors, swallowing girls.

And through the rising smoke we see
the pale outlines of 4 pink musicians
bringing on the 13th Technicolor Dream
the flip side of the Sgt. Pepper kaleidoscope.

But while the piper performs, his spirit
crawls to the corner of the Universe

The last exhibit in the Museum Of Sound
is a room of stripes swallowed in time.
Don't blink, or you'll miss the Mellotron maiden
        ~ escape the liquid mirror ~
pursued by a black and green scarecrow
|S|P|I|T|T|I|N|G| |T|O|O|T|H|P|I|C|K|S|.

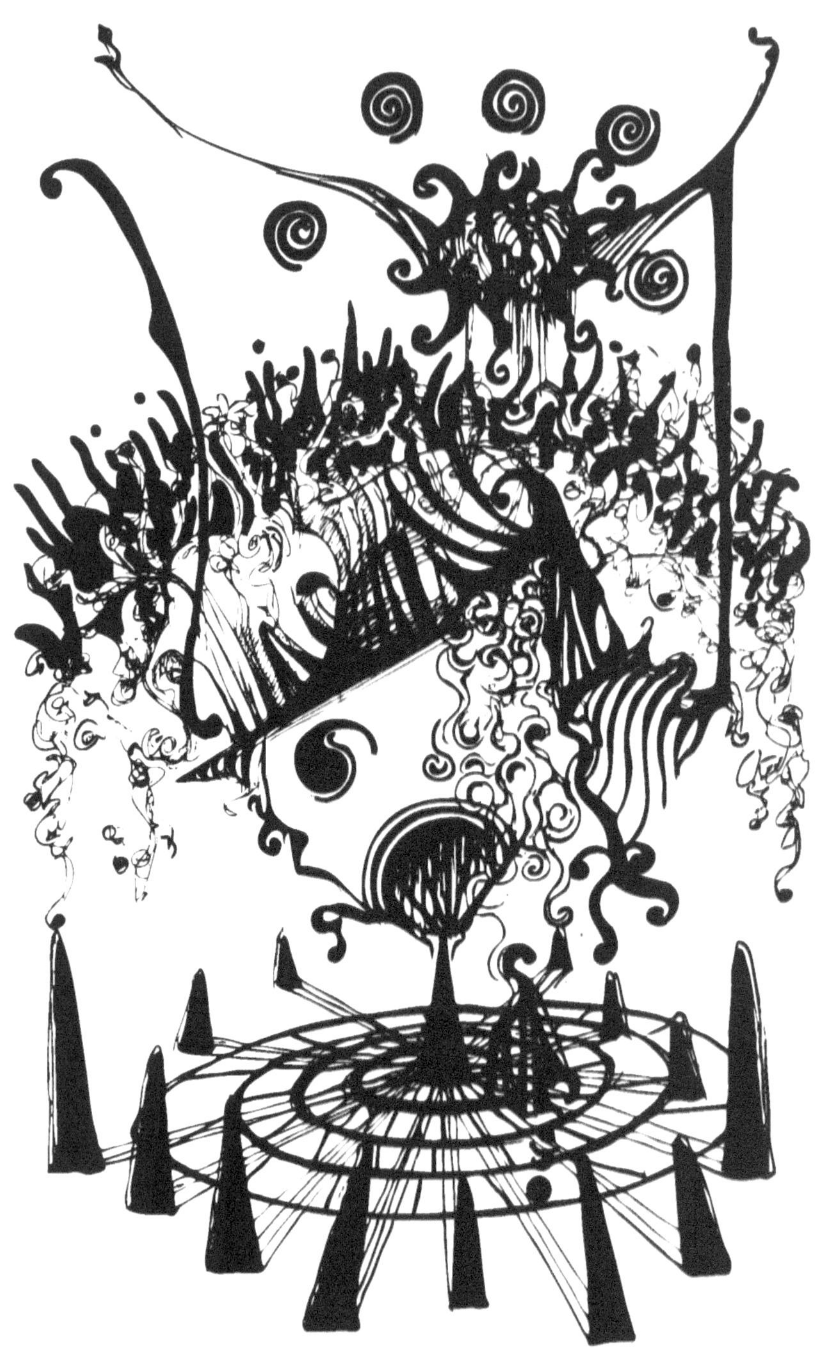

33 Little Girls Set Out To Hunt The White Butterfly

-for Max Ernst

Perturbation, my sisters.
The day weighs heavy on our shoulders.
Take up your nets, for we wander ever-hungry
like discarded pets into the horizon
where the sun never sets.

Thirty-three little mouths whispering
  `collecting time!'

The forest consumes memory
but the butterflies are thicker here, you see.
Sisters steal about angelically
(dresses collapsing slowly)
the jellyfish descend into the meadow's green sea
three-times-ten-plus-three.

If he should return to this place
braid your hair in his shoelaces.
The moon will chase the white butterfly
that huddles in our pale chests
around and around the black house mother
until the days walk backward
and the moon retracts its glowing eyelid
and a butterfly of man's hands
visits our constellation of windowsills
with a flower on every fingernail.

Sisters, The White eludes us.
It avoids the garden aeroplane traps
disdains the snow flowers
flying with the blind eyes of silence.

Like fathers, it is elusive and fickle,
but we will find it before the dawn.

`Today, in the time of no shepherds,
a lost flock of giddy goats got lost
under the cocoons of Sedona.
Last spotted near Grasshopper Point,
washing their bodies in wild rivers,
the current overtook them, and their shoulders
become butterflies, carrying their sad and sweet
song away with the wind.'

We are maidens learning to mend
We are the nests for future men
The world shall know nothing of us
Here in the land of cicadas
Here in the land of droning violins.

Hamburgers Fries Coffee & Gasoline

Hamburgers fries coffee & gasoline
the service station huddles behind the road sign.
Truckers roll on down the interstate
big metal geese of honking song
`cuz out on the asphalt the trucker roams free
gasoline hamburgers fries & coffee.

They laid that ladder down
and it grew into train tracks,
so hop aboard with the hobo blues man.
   `Share yer soup, be loose with yer change
   the sheltering train keeps us out of the rain.
   Sing yer song and gnaw yer bone
   til the Lord reaches down
   and takes us all home.'

Gasfoodlodging gasfoodlodging
climbing clouds crowd up the sky
marmalade light turning morning to night.
And all those little prairie doggies
pop their heads high out the hole houses.

Starlight on the cacti
moonlight in the canyon
thunderstorms hide flickering stars
comet tails make sparking worms
lightning splinters, dancing knives
raindrop bees down heaven's hives.

Flashing lights strobe over the plains
cracking in vertical rivers, the rains flood
the seats of an abandoned Chevy Impala
asleep in rust, dripping midnight.

The storm, despotic, batters the hood
dripdropdripdrop wasteland rest stop.

Stick figures roam cave walls
boulders watch the tumbleweeds
the humpty dumpty wicker steeds
rolling wild like billiard shots.

Inching insects in sunrise blankets
humming, marching, serenading
collecting up the twigs and trinkets
herding the seconds of morning.

The wind's melodeon cry
the rising sun in the scaffolding sky
lighting this rusting industrial scene
  off the Bear Tooth Highway
  in the Great Horn Basin
where the land reaches out vast and lean
hamburgers fries coffee & gasoline.

Mediocrity

They first discovered it buried deep in forgotten tombs, faint glowing cinders. But there was nothing left to burn in those caves of sorrow, so enterprising jackals built shrines where it could burn forever.

The shrines were called televisions, and were hypnotic, mystical forges of the dark arts that melted images, so many images copulating in furious speed that the peasants could not keep up, cornered animals clawing in their minds to get out.

Trapped in this narcotic prism of lights, their hearts slowed down and their hunger became voyeurism.

Soon, the peasants themselves became actors, but the play was neither tragic nor comedic, but a never arriving elevator packed with shrieking mannequins demanding their spotlight in the image forge. The elevator moved backward through time, and all the wisdom that humanity died for washed over it, polishing the steel into a careening jewel.

Listen. Inside the elevator there was nothing but filth. Filthy lies and filthy ringmasters beckoning young actors like leaping dogs. The entire human race spun around and around in that gleaming elevator ship on a path so endless that no one realized it was a spiral.

The seeping, flickering images flooded the elevator where the peasants fought, and the day finally came when their mind animals died, and all that was left were shells, shells that were once human, shells that cracked

and turned to dust in forgotten tombs,
faint glowing cinders.

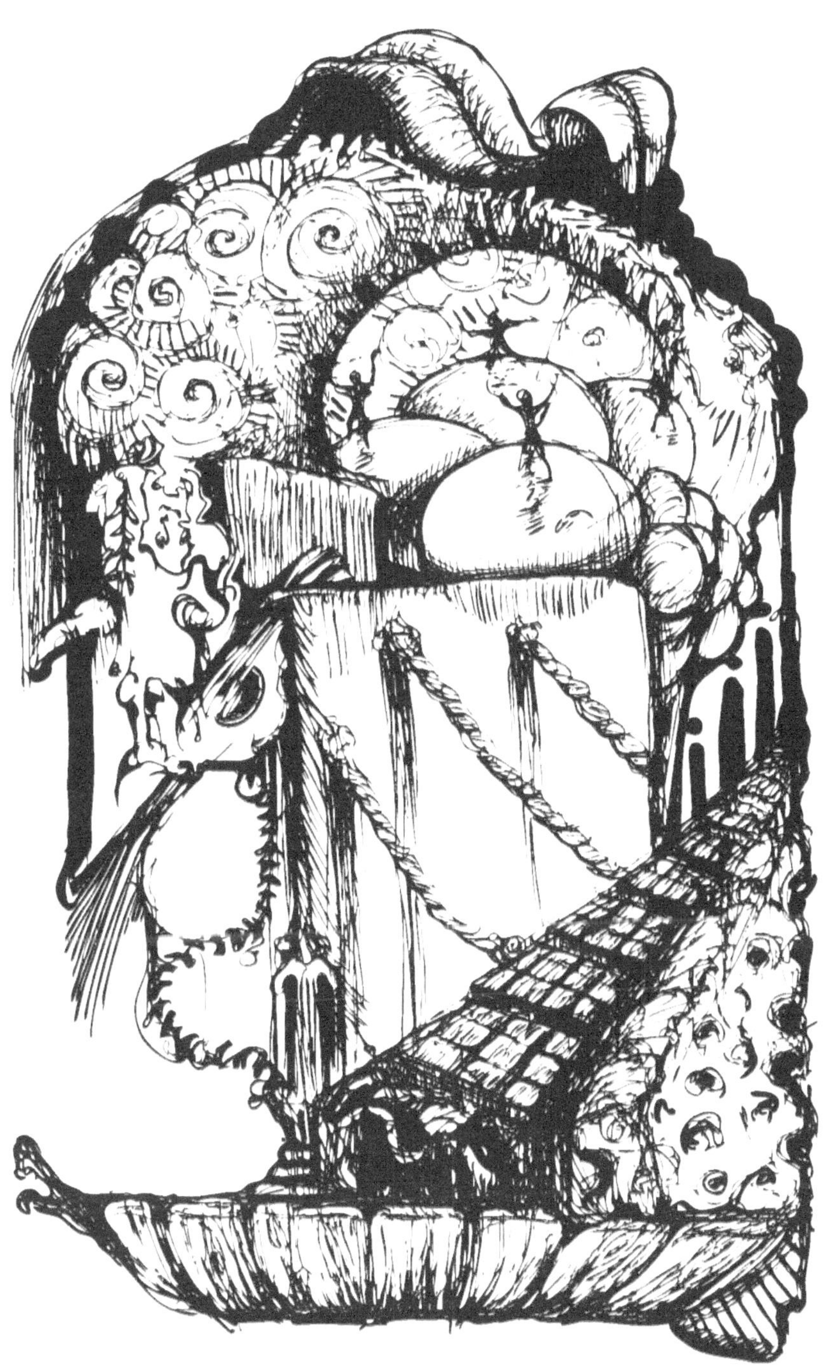

The Lost Monologue From The Final 20 Minutes Of Stanley Kubrick's 2001

HAL has deceived me, but the Universe receives me.

~ Is this my mission? ~

I vibrate unwillingly,   spasmodically...
I am unfamiliar with your emerald oceans
becoming rainbows, the rushing dawn
revealing the chromatic
iris of the Universe.

I spill my HURTLING spacecraft into the center
of your cosmic infancy.
I am Bowman, The Archer!
SHOT LIKE HUMAN SHRAPNEL through
your fireworks of infinity.

Ancient astral deserts of blue, violet and electric orange
flattened, flooding valleys filter dimwitted understanding.

My eyes eat information,
but my mind is FULL.
This knowledge engulfs me, I am vermin.
Afterbirth constellations ignore me like a trivial star
but I become younger through wonder
child of space in a mother embrace
cobalt lakes spill red desert wounds
eyebrow cliffs of the vertical man
NO ONE HAS SEEN WHAT I NOW SEE.

The math becoming crystals
the skies that are plains of distance with no matter
the colors painting galaxies

I am frightened, memory vomiting reason.
If I blink, all is lost, and fear will only unravel
the travel behind me. Speed is my life now,
how long can this last?

I long
    for the beach
        of lost sand
                after an everlasting sea.

And it is here -

*   *   *

NOW!

(PANTING HORROR OF PRIMAL DISBELIEF)

A French drawing room.
I KNOW
I'm an experiment now.

Why these bluish walls growing
        from glowing floors?
I look at my pod, though I don't remember
        getting out of it. A strange, round prop
    for this elegant prison.

I stroll each domestic exhibition in dragging death,
my mind reeling, my spacesuit unnecessary, though
 I cling to it, binding me to familiarity in these rooms
of annihilation.

(The day I took it off I died,
                but my future continued,
        poured out daily into a perfect crystal glass
                like fine, red mortality.
        And with every breath
                        passes a new eternity).

Each moment I cling to the previous one,
                for time doesn't know me anymore,
        and I've stopped looking in the mirror
for fear of eating my own death.

        The sink doesn't change,
                the bed doesn't change,
        the floor is blank, screaming, infinitely white.
                The food appears, as before.
        I am feeding, I have fed, I will feed again.

I attempt to carve meaning with my eyes,
                but they are spent, incredulous,
                        dull like prison spoons
from arduous, impossible work.

*   *   *

Something has changed recently.
                I no longer look - there is nothing to see.
                        I breathe deeply, evenly, intentionally...
and eventually there is civility. Accepting rationally
                        what I've become,
                a peeling fruit in Eden's maze.

My bedroom is regal yet bland, focused into being
by some unseen intelligence. The checkerboard floor
does not know where to play me, and I think I may be

an idle game for some unknown God
who has moved onto other toys.
And I slip exhausted into the warm
womb of capitulation.

But oh my God in heaven,
don't keep me out
once my ending is written!

I was a simple scientist with a glass face, afflicted with
outer space. This scene is now my life, a wife of finite
days. But no miracle can preserve my draining minutes,
no faucet is tight enough.

So I exist in casual refinement, as death follows
in slow motion, reaching from the future
with the grasping hands of an insatiable clock.

Alone, lost in my thoughts, one day I am aware of my
younger self looking at me from behind, surveying my
graying head. I go to him eagerly,
but he disappears,
every time.

I reach for the salt and the glass falls from the table
and breaks. The glass *b-r-e-a-k-s,* it is broken.

Can illusions break?

No matter, the wine today is better than before,
and I feel something is coming.
I was blessed, of course, and I know now
that my time is near,
because there's a man lying there in hobbled finality
and I see that it is my grandfather, I.

*   *   *

I can no longer get up from my bed.
   I am tired of waiting, of living.

                              No transformations left.
            end this

finish your game

                                    not long now

        It is HERE, towering over my bed
like an ancient friend. I fly gratefully into its black gaze.

A T L A S T

I
am
a
child
again
and
I
can
finally
exit
my
own
film.

Map Of The Immortals

WHY DOES THIS SICKNESS PERVADE YOUR MIND?
You as a child were cut from the crystal of perfection,
can you not see that fear, want and suffering is *learned*
from a thousand trials flowing from the pen of your
jailor?

A searchlight scans the seas for life, while you play at
greatness in an orchestra performing on a ship lost at
sea. But this was *never* your ship. You aren't a guest
and you *don't have a ticket.* Drop the violin and dive into
the murky black depths, this is what life is for, powering
mightily against the current while krakens of conformity
feel through the darkness at your kicking feet.

> *This dangerous, kinetic reality is infinitely more*
> *desirable than a splintering voyage performing*
> *for a crowd of disinterested strangers.*

AND IF PERFECTION IS YOUR DESIGN
why ply your temple with snake-oil serums, or slick
the fur of the beast of industry with your golden life
essence? Only while *rushing* can a river ward off
putrefaction. Mosquitos seek stagnation, but the dead
pool does not *create* them. And parasitical thoughts
grow from the stagnation of indecision.

> *If cancer is the language of acid,*
> *do not provide an arena for its deadly performance.*
> *Return your body to the garden.*
> *Give back what was lost.*

Don't mistake a weed for a beanstalk, or build your
castles on the turrets of ruins.

It is on the FOUNDATION where you must toil,
everything else is fragile artifice.

AND WHY PUNISH THE BABE IN YOUR SOUL
over and over, with the lashing whips of self-doubt?
Your soul is an infinite foundry of lights, not a straw hut
ravaged by winds, withering in obscurity, scattering
it's structure across the beach of the cemetery.

Glaciers of thought
melt unnoticed
in the ocean of routine.

The diagram of your spirit is in 5 densities, and the
speed of light is slow-motion to the communication
of entangled particles. And we are ALL entangled
my friend. Beauty is instantaneous, and there
ARE NO STREETLIGHTS in the realm of the infinite.

Heed well these last three lines,
Grass doesn't strain to grow,
birds didn't invent flight,
and the Sun doesn't need a light switch.

French Vodka And The Quantum Age

Did you know that French vodka
utilizes zig-zagging glass tubes
feeding extraordinary contraptions
milling wheat to a fine powder
sieved in remarkable vibrating machines
and married with the water of deep limestone wells
de-mineralized by double-reverse osmosis
corkscrewing downward counter-clockwise
into a dizzying vortex of grey mist
bottled in etched glass and streamed into goblets
effectively making hangovers obsolete?

This I think, is a fine use for science.

Long ago, in the war of a thousand tears, the elders
surmised that terrorism was more like reaction poverty
than invented evil, and that if they truly wanted to end
it, they must invite it into the kitchen.

This ushered in a golden quantum age. The Manhattan,
Mai Tai and Martini commanded the genius of the
downsized molecular fizzicist previously mixing
cannibal cocktails for wall-faced generals, stiff and
starchly gray, who themselves were demoted to avatars
for mayhem simulations.

(Hell, even they had enough). `If we aren't killing
hostiles anymore, I'm watching the game,'
they harrumphed.

While epic poems were composed over waves of
meringue, the machines hesitated at the front and
wondered if *their* time wasn't better spent in astronomy,

for even machines have dreams, electric though they are,
and filled with chromatic waves of frequency.

*This hesitation startled the napalm peasants,
peeking from thatched shacks and shuddering
in disbelief. And perhaps it was then that they
realized that war is just a bad dream whispered
into the ear of a sleeping man, and when the man
wakes, the dream dies, and is no more.*

`Let's not speak of it again,' the soldier cautioned, biting
into a chocolate-dipped macaroon. `Even the greatest
villain of the cinema needs belief to survive, for belief is
the engine of creation, and no plane can bomb a city
without an engine.'

Street Manifesto

ALL I EVER WANTED TO BE WAS IDEAS
A beat-up book in trembling hands, a bluebird flying
through the businessman's ears, record shop in the shade
shouting Hendrix into city sidewalks, black leather mutant smile
wildfires and a dagger manifesto, fruit trees suffocating factories
the long white wail of a seagull leaving the city for the tropics
growling motorcycles, summer street festival, onebuckbeerstand
sunburnt neck, the shape of a girl in a dress, doves flying from
top hats into an orchestra of skeletons, a chorus of justice
at city hall, free growing armies with hand-made
picket signs defeating

TELEVISIONS

bullhorn of brutality
Vs.
mad freezing humanity screaming
NEVER AGAIN!
NEVER AGAIN!
NEVER AGAIN!
I AM FROM THE TRIBE OF SILVER BLOOD CHILDREN
Black mind, wild eyes, heir to the throne the tyrants shun
born in a wormhole of crashing suns, built from bones wrought
from passion, animal champion negator of fashion, creator of fine
forest shrines in rhyme, shooting sunshine, riding vines, Viking
brawn with a back of mountains bearing tonnage of truth ore
a tall troubadour serenading crows in prose, the peace
train conductor of the peasant race shooting off
the tracks into the gaping cracks of
CONFORMITY'S FACE
| | | | | | | | | | | |
! AND WE ALL SCREAM !
I WILL NOT BURN IN ANOTHER MAN'S TORCH!
I WILL USE MY MIND TO REMAKE THE WORLD!

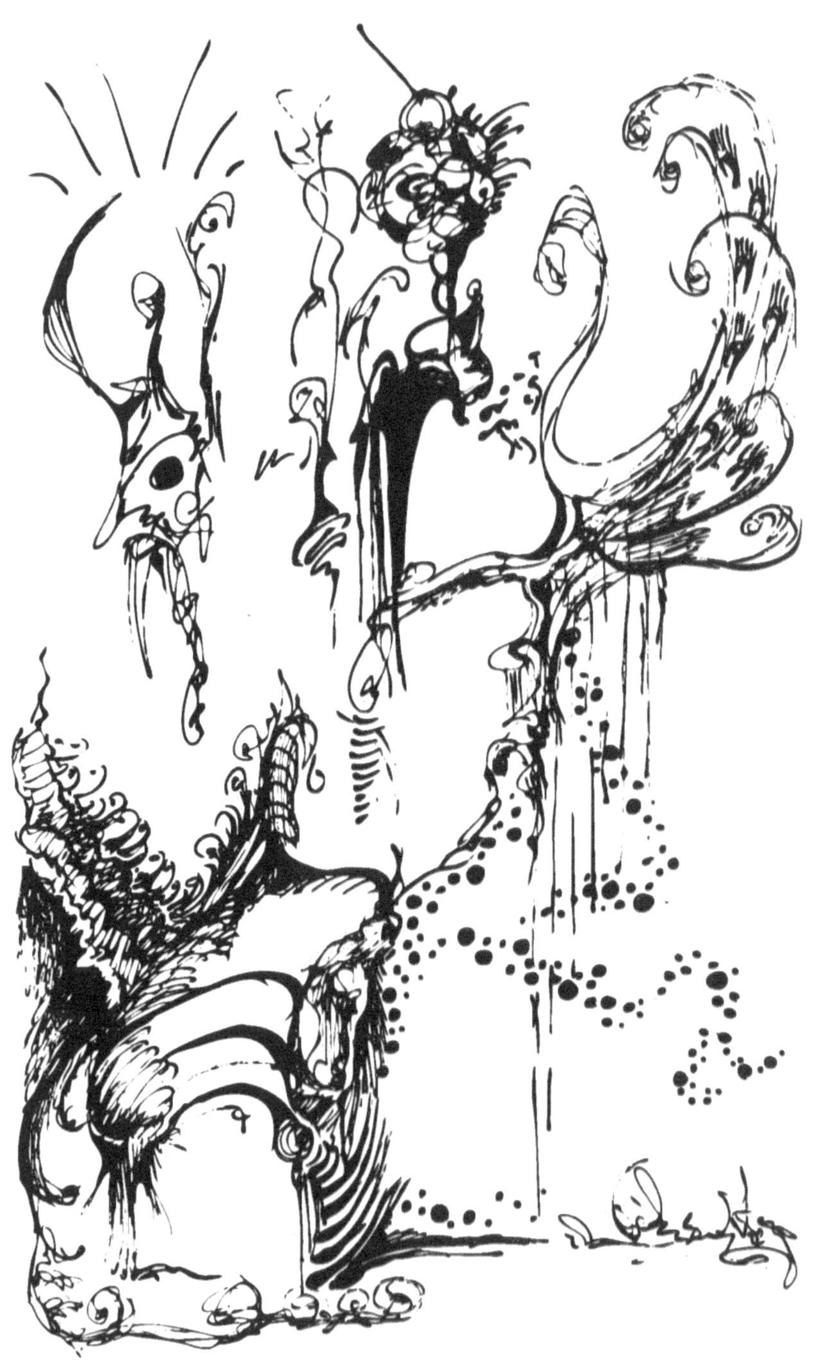

Clouds

And if our world is an Eden of mist
these are teams of white mustangs
vast precipitation buffaloes
high racing caravans
billowing beasts of breath.

Pale trudging giants
harnessed to waterfalls
drifting in the sunset
hunkering down in the mountains
snowing pelts on green haunches.

Lonesome landscapes
speaking in plumes of loss.

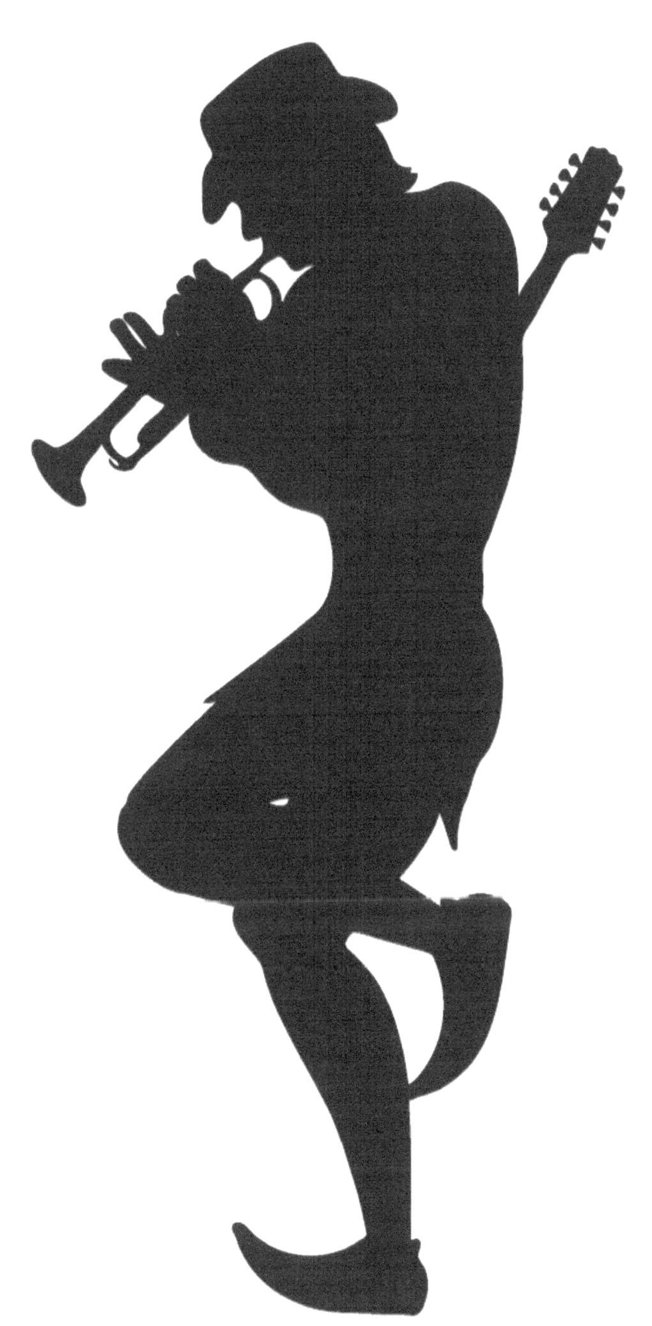

About The Author

E. P. Mattson is a native Californian poet and multi-disciplinary artist. His work is keenly concerned with inner transformation, the supreme authority of the individual over the collective, and the profound healing power of the arts and the natural world.

In his professional life he's worked as an artist on everything from theatrical plays, to video games, to blockbuster Hollywood films. But after many years of collaboration, he is now focusing on his personal artistic works, following the white rabbit of the spirit during these astounding times of transformation and upheaval.

Currently, he's at work on a book of travel poetry, a collection of short plays, and the follow-up to *The Opulence Of Invention*. Learn more at *epmattson.com*.

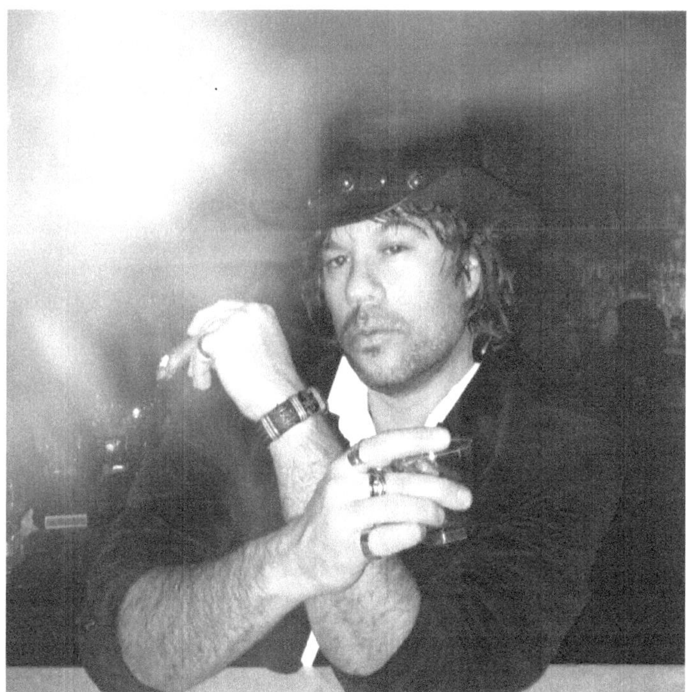